CYBERSAFETY

Internet Addiction and Online Gaming

CYBER**SAFETY**

CYBERSAFETY

Internet Addiction and Online Gaming

SAMUEL C. MCQUADE, III, PH.D.,
SARAH E. GENTRY, AND JAMES P. COLT, ED. D.

MARCUS K. ROGERS, PH.D.,
CONSULTING EDITOR

CHELSEA HOUSE
An Infobase Learning Company

Chelsea House
An Infobase Learning Company
132 West 31st Street
New York NY 10001

Library of Congress Cataloging-in-Publication Data

McQuade, Samuel C.
  Internet addiction and online gaming / Samuel C. McQuade III, Sarah E. Gentry, and James P. Colt ; consulting editor, Marcus K. Rogers.
     p. cm. -- (Cybersafety)
  Includes bibliographical references and index.
  ISBN-13: 978-1-60413-696-8 (hardcover : alk. paper)
  ISBN-10: 1-60413-696-0 (hardcover : alk. paper) 1. Internet addiction--Popular works. 2. Video game addiction--Popular works. I. Gentry, Sarah. II. Colt, James P. III. Rogers, Marcus K. IV. Title.
  RC569.5.I54M37 2011
  616.85'84--dc22

                    2011005645

Chelsea House books are available at special discounts when purchased in bulk quantities for businesses, associations, institutions, or sales promotions. Please call our Special Sales Department in New York at (212) 967-8800 or (800) 322-8755.

You can find Chelsea House on the World Wide Web at http://www.infobaselearning.com

Text design by Erik Lindstrom
Cover design by Takeshi Takahashi
Composition by Kerry Casey
Cover printed by Yurchak Printing, Landisville, Pa.
Book printed and bound by Yurchak Printing, Landisville, Pa..
Date printed: March 2012

Printed in the United States of America

This book is printed on acid-free paper.

All links and Web addresses were checked and verified to be correct at the time of publication. Because of the dynamic nature of the Web, some addresses and links may have changed since publication and may no longer be valid.

CONTENTS

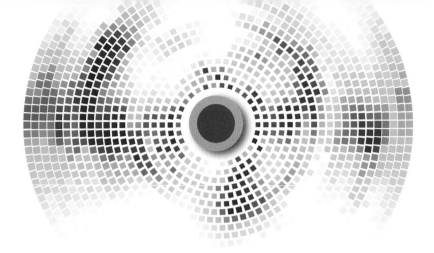

Foreword

The Internet has had and will continue to have a profound effect on society. It is hard to imagine life without such technologies as computers, cell phones, gaming devices, and so on. The Internet, World Wide Web, and their associated technologies have altered our social and personal experience of the world. In no other time in history have we had such access to knowledge and raw information. One can search the Library of Congress, the Louvre in Paris, and read online books and articles or watch videos from just about any country in the world. We can interact and chat with friends down the street, in another state, or halfway around the globe. The world is now our neighborhood. We are a "wired" society that lives a significant amount of our life online and tethered to technology.

The Internet, or cyberspace, is a great enabler. What is also becoming apparent, though, is that there is a dark side to this global wired society. As the concept of who our friends are moves from real world relationships to cyberspace connections, so also do the rules change regarding social conventions and norms. How many friends do we have online that we have actually met in person? Are online-only friends even real or at the very least whom they claim to be? We also begin to redefine privacy. Questions arise over what should be considered private or public information. Do we really want every-one in the global society to have access to our personal information? As with the real world there may be people online that we do not wish to associate with or grant access to our lives.

It is easy to become enamored with technology and the technol-ogy/information revolution. It is equally as easy to become paranoid about the dangers inherent in cyberspace. What is difficult but neces-sary is to be realistic about how our world has been forever changed. We see numerous magazine, TV, and newspaper headlines regarding the latest cybercrime attacks. Stories about identity theft being the fastest growing nonviolent criminal activity are common. The govern-ment is concerned with cyber or information warfare attacks against critical infrastructures. Given this kind of media coverage it is easy to think that the sky is falling and cyberspace is somehow evil. Yet if we step back and think about it, technology is neither good nor bad, it simply *is*. Technology is neutral; it is what we do with technology that determines whether it improves our lives or damages and makes our lives more difficult. Even if someone is on the proverbial fence over whether the Internet and cyberspace are society enablers or disablers, what is certain is that the technology genie is out of the bottle. We will never be able to put it back in; we need to learn how to master and live with it.

Learning to live with the Internet and its technological offshoots is one of the objectives behind the Cybersafety series of books. The immortal words of Sir Francis Bacon (the father of the scientific method), "knowledge is power," ring especially true today. If we live in a society that is dependent on technology and therefore we live a significant portion of our daily lives in cyberspace, then we need to understand the potential downside as well as the upside. However, what is not useful is fear mongering or the demonization of technology.

There is no doubt that cyberspace has its share of bad actors and criminals. This should not come as a surprise to anyone. Cyberspace mirrors traditional society, including both the good and unfortunately the bad. Historically criminals have been attracted to new technologies in an effort to improve and extend their criminal methods. The same advantages that technology and cyberspace bring to our normal everyday lives (e.g., increased communication, the ability to remotely access information) can be used in a criminal manner. Online fraud, identity theft, cyberstalking, and cyberbullying are but a few of the ugly behaviors that we see online today.

Navigating successfully through cyberspace also means that we need to understand how the "cyber" affects our personality and social behavior. One of the empowering facets of cyberspace and technology is the fact that we can escape reality and find creative outlets for ourselves. We can immerse ourselves in computer and online games, and if so inclined, satisfy our desire to gamble or engage in other risky behaviors. The sense of anonymity and the ability to redefine who we are online can be intoxicating to some people. We can experiment with new roles and behaviors that may be polar opposites of who we are in the real physical world. Yet, as in the real world, our activities and behaviors in cyberspace have consequences too. Well-meaning escapism can turn to online addictions; seemingly harmless distractions like online gaming can consume so much of our time that our real world relationships and lives are negatively affected. The presumed anonymity afforded by cyberspace can lead to bullying and stalking, behaviors that can have a profound and damaging impact on the victims and on ourselves.

The philosophy behind the Cybersafety series is based on the recognition that cyberspace and technology will continue to play an increasingly important part of our everyday lives. The way in which we define who we are, our home life, school, social relationships, and work life will all be influenced and impacted by our online behaviors and misbehaviors. Our historical notions of privacy will also be redefined in terms of universal access to our everyday activities and posted musings. The Cybersafety series was created to assist us in understanding and making sense of the online world. The intended audience for the series is those individuals who are and will be the most directly affected by cyberspace and its technologies, namely young people (i.e., those in grades 6 -12).

Young people are the future of our society. It is they who will go forward and shape societal norms, customs, public policy, draft new laws, and be our leaders. They will be tasked with developing positive coping mechanisms for both the physical and cyberworlds. They will have dual citizenship responsibilities: citizens of the physical and of the cyber. It is hoped that this series will assist in providing insight, guidance, and positive advice for this journey.

The series is divided into books that logically gather related concepts and issues. The goal of each book in the series is not to scare but to educate and inform the reader. As the title of the series states the focus is on "safety." Each book in the series provides advice on what to watch out for and how to be safer. The emphasis is on education and awareness while providing a frank discussion related to the consequences of certain online behaviors.

It is my sincere pleasure and honor to be associated with this series. As a former law enforcement officer and current educator, I am all too aware of the dangers that can befall our young people. I am also keenly aware that young people are more astute than some adults commonly give them credit for being. Therefore it is imperative that we begin a dialogue that enhances our awareness and encourages and challenges the reader to reexamine their behaviors and attitudes toward cyberspace and technology. We fear what we do not understand; fear is not productive, but knowledge is empowering. So let's begin our collective journey into arming ourselves with more knowledge.

—Marcus K. Rogers, Ph.D., CISSP, DFCP,
Founder and Director,
Cyber Forensics Program,
Purdue University

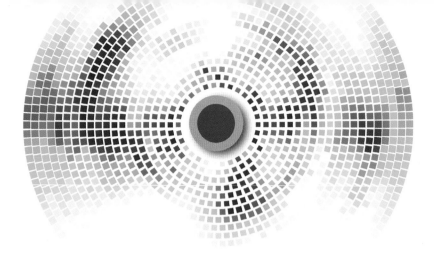

Introduction

"Can one desire too much of a good thing?"
Shakespeare, *As You Like It,* Act IV, Scene I

The Internet is a really cool environment in which to work and play. People use the Internet for personal things, to do schoolwork, and at their jobs. Using the Net is especially popular among young people who, in computerized countries like the United States of America, often begin using computers and the Internet during their preschool or kindergarten years. Research shows that the very first form of social computing that youth engage in is online gaming. As people age they also learn how to use computers and portable information technology (IT) devices, such as cell phones, to browse the Web, check e-mail, instant message, and create Web profiles that aid them in staying in touch with friends and family.

The joy, allure, thrill, risk, entertainment, and other excitement associated with many online activities can also lead to overuse. If not held in check, use of online activities may steadily increase to become an *obsession*—something a person feels like they *must* do. Over time if an obsession is not stopped or balanced with other activities in a person's life, it will command unhealthy amounts of attention, time, or money. This is true for off-line and online forms of obsessions.

Eventually an obsession comes to dominate a person's thinking and infringe upon a person's time and responsibilities. Obsessions in some people rise to the level of becoming an *addiction*—a habitual or compulsive behavior. Addictions are usually associated with harmful behaviors that negatively affect one or more aspects of a person's life. An addict is a person who has an addiction. Being an addict does not make someone a bad person. Addicts are considered sick and in need of medical and psychological treatment. Yet an addict's addiction often has negative effects on family members, friends, or coworkers. Consequently, addiction in all its forms is a societal concern.

When an obsession involves online activity, excessive amounts of computer or cell phone activity become dominant and then harmful in a person's life. This condition is commonly referred to as "Internet addiction." People with Internet addiction compulsively spend unusual amounts of time online playing games, chatting, browsing, or doing other things to the detriment of their school-work or jobs.

Consider the following account based on a true story. A 36-year-old man was unemployed and homeless for most of his life. He slept in a tent on top of three discarded mattresses he had found somewhere. He owned very little. He had no place to shower or properly wash his clothes. His daily routine began with getting up whenever he wanted, walking to a store, and using government food stamps to buy a microwave meal he could heat up in the store. When he had no money or food stamps, he went to a community soup kitchen for a free meal. Typically the man walked to a local state university computer lab that was open to the public. There he spent hours upon hours each day using a computer to engage in a role-playing video game (usually *World of Warcraft*). Alternatively he browsed Web sites or blogs to pass the time away. When the lab closed for

Young children are usually first exposed to the Internet through online gaming. Overuse of online activities, such as social networking or playing video games, can lead to Internet addiction. *(Source: AP Photo/Elaine Thompson)*

the day, he wandered the city streets and eventually returned to his tent to sleep. One time the homeless man received a laptop from relatives. It enabled him to stay connected to the Internet from any location in the city with free Wi-Fi. Although never officially diagnosed as being addicted to the Internet, the man had admitted to all classical signs of being addicted—especially a deep feeling of needing to be online and becoming restless when he was not. In thinking back the man realized that his need to be online and inability to stay focused on real-world things led to his dropping out of school, not holding a job, and eventually becoming homeless. His brother, a journalist who wrote about Internet addiction, feared the man's homelessness would lead him to an early death by exposing him to weather, sickness, and crime.[1] He contacted a social worker to get help for his brother. Perhaps through treatment his homeless brother could once again become a healthy student and productive worker with a real home.

For a moment, think about how daily routines of many people involve relying on computers or other types of IT devices such as computers and cell phones. For most people, a personal computer or cell phone is simply a tool that helps them to communicate. Though vital in their lives, using an IT device or being connected to the Internet is not crucial to their sense of well-being. In other words, few people become distraught or overly distressed when they cannot go online. For most people, using IT devices and the Internet merely increases convenience and productivity in communicating. People afflicted with Internet addiction, however, feel compelled to be online for the sake of being online and doing what they enjoy most, even if it causes harm in other aspects of their lives.

IT devices and the Net enable people to do many things at once and be very productive. This is true even if within a given instant people can focus on only one thing at a time. Individuals use the Internet for myriad reasons, including to: play games or engage in other forms of entertainment, conduct research, socialize, manage household or business affairs, or even to escape from the real world as when daydreaming. None of these activities or specific levels of engagement is inherently harmful. Each can have little rewards that pioneering social scientist B.F. Skinner recognized as a shaping process in which people learn and continue doing things they enjoy. For some Internet users, online rewards become powerful incentives, but also dangerous with regard to potential harm realized through neglected real-life relationships and responsibilities. Routine interconnections and productivity afforded through the Internet are good, but they are not good for people who feel *compelled* to be online in order to play games, interact, or view certain kinds of alluring content. For most people, Internet activities and online gaming are a wonderful form of recreation having little if anything to do with addiction, but for some they can become a serious problem.

To learn about online gaming and the dangers of Internet addiction, it is important to consider how computer devices enable and affect everyday lives. It is also important for safe and responsible users of IT devices and the Internet to consider how to make sound decisions about what they choose to view and do online. Users must learn to confront the allure of technology-enabled communications, interactions, and content to determine when things are enjoyable or productive versus becoming excessive and harmful to their real lives off-line.

Deciding what and how much of something online is good or not can be a challenge. This is because individual users have different views about what kinds of content they find interesting or valuable relative to how much time they have to view it during an online session, in the course of their day, or in their lives overall. The point at which using the Internet to view particular kinds of content becomes problematic differs among users—what is problematic for one user may not be for another. It is natural and generally healthy for Internet users to spend relatively small amounts of time exploring new things online and also communicating. They do this out of curiosity and genuine desire to learn, and to have fun and stay connected with friends and family. This is normal in the course of social networking, online gaming, doing research for school assignments, or shopping online. Some users, however, develop a desire to view or engage in certain things to a point of insatiability. Never being completely satisfied, they spend hours upon hours clicking away at icons and images in an effort to achieve ever-increasing levels of joy only to become tired and only marginally happy. Over time they need to spend more and more time to achieve the same or higher levels of satisfaction. Eventually they spend so much time online they neglect other things and responsibilities of life. What began with simple curiosity became a bad habit that caused significant problems in their lives.

There is a reason why digital devices, like BlackBerries, are sometimes referred to as "crackberries," referring to the addictive nature of crack cocaine, and why the names of some popular online games are distorted (e.g., "World of Warcrack" instead of *World of Warcraft* or "NeverRest" instead of *EverQuest).* These games and many like them are so alluring to some players that they have trouble stopping any given session. Before they know it they have spent hours playing nonstop to win a game that may be designed to be unwinnable!

The nature of addiction is indefinite. There are many ways that it comes about, numerous factors contribute to it, and it causes a range of harm in peoples' lives. A solid understanding of these factors is required to avoid common pitfalls of ignorance embodied in dismissive expressions like, "Oh, it's just Internet addiction." While many people casually joke about becoming "addicted to Facebook" or to their cell phones or other Internet devices, such statements usually refer to people who use their devices regularly without experiencing any real personal problems. However, if a person's normal life is harmed or compromised in some way, they may be experiencing effects of addiction and be in need of professional assistance. True understanding of online and Internet addiction can aid people in becoming alert for and sensitive to its causes and harms. This will allow them to help people in need and to avoid poor choices in their own lives so that they do not obsessively engage in unhealthy behaviors.

This book can help by asking and answering several important questions:

- What is Internet addiction, and what are the characteristics and causes of such addiction?
- How much Internet addiction is there in society and in what ways does it occur (e.g., online gaming, gambling, social networking, shopping, or viewing sexual content)?
- How much online gaming (or off-line electronic gaming) is too much?
- What kinds of computer devices, Internet content, and online interactions, including but not limited to online gaming, can take over a person's life and cause them problems?
- Is using a cell phone safer than using a computer in order to prevent becoming addicted?
- In what ways are people harmed when they become addicted to online things?
- Who else suffers, and in what ways, when a friend or loved one becomes addicted to the Internet?
- What, if any, connections exist between online addiction and crime?
- What educational programs or health services exist to help users who use the Net excessively?
- What can children and their parents, teachers, and other community members do to help prevent Internet addiction from occurring?

These questions represent major subjects to be explored in this book.

Chapter 1 defines addiction and Internet addiction, and will explore types and characteristics of online addicts, along with the causes of addiction.

Chapter 2 explores social computing and online addiction.

Chapter 3 describes the hugely popular online gaming phenomenon and the potential for addiction with gaming.

Chapter 4 provides an overview of online gambling and addiction issues that are associated with it.

Chapter 5 documents additional digital addictions, including excessive use of mobile devices, compulsive shopping, and Internet pornography.

Chapter 6 examines and describes the associated dangers and harmful aspects of computing and Internet addiction.

Chapter 7 offers advice to help young people practice safe and responsible computing.

Regardless of ongoing scientific debate about the validity of so-called Internet addiction, as a practical matter some users of IT devices and the Internet suffer from excessive use of these technologies. Obsessing about online activities or content in ways that compromise long-term joy or productivity is harmful. Children, especially those who are poorly educated about the Internet or unsupervised online are especially vulnerable to developing impulsive, obsessive, and addictive behaviors.

Internet addiction may overlap with other forms of addiction, such as dependency on drugs or alcohol. People who experience harmful effects from excessive engagement in one area of their life (such as online gaming or excessive consumption of drugs or alcohol) are more likely susceptible to becoming addicted to more than one thing. Some people seem to be naturally more prone to addiction than others, and individuals vary in their ability to cope with addictions and kick obsessive or unhealthy habits. Yet professional assistance, when available, is valuable for a majority of people with any form of addiction. People genuinely suffer from the addiction(s) they experience, including Internet addiction, and so do their friends, family, and coworkers.

The urge to be online anywhere or anytime may become very strong, much like a craving for certain foods or substances. Differences between enjoyment, obsession, and addiction vary among people such that it is often unclear when feelings of reward cross into feelings of having to be online. Knowing where these boundaries are with regard to the amount of time spent online and level of intensity of engagement relative to other things that matter is extremely important for individuals to consider in order to make smart and reasonable decisions for using technology.

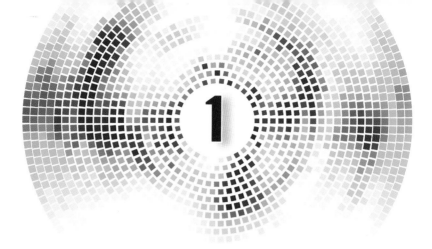

Addiction and Internet Addiction

The Internet seemed like a lot of fun for Shelly. She spent countless hours chatting with friends online, sending jokes, and getting the latest scoop on her favorite stars. Shelly also discovered online communities and forums and she was really into downloading music. As a news junkie Shelly could not wait to get online to find out what was going on in the world. Her online activities became even more exciting when she discovered eBay and all the great things she could buy online, but before long her credit cards were maxed out. Shelly was so preoccupied with being online, though, that she really didn't care about her finances and other important things in her life, not even when her boyfriend gave up on her because all she wanted to do was to be online.

Shelly was also a mother who periodically, and in small ways, began to neglect her two young school-aged children. The Internet became the center of her life and she was always considering new ways or excuses to get back online. Sometimes she would wake up and immediately get online while her kids waited for breakfast or got on their school bus by themselves. Because she was always on the Internet, her house became so neglected that it was hard to walk through it. The bathrooms were filthy, and dirty dishes and laundry piled up to a point that the washer and dryer were no longer visible. It was then that she discovered the games that could be played online. Shelly played and played and played. She played at work on her company's computer and after nearly losing her job still continued to play.

Eventually Shelly met someone online and began to fall in love. She discovered, however, that the man had been married for 26 years and was just goofing around! She decided to take a break from the Internet and spoke with a counselor at work. It was then that she realized that she was addicted. She later reflected, "The Internet is a marvelous, mind-boggling thing but it is seductive. It can be an addiction and it can wreck your life if you don't get it in check."[1]

Addiction is a condition in which a person becomes dependent on a substance or activity to such an extent that they experience trauma in their lives or as a consequence of attempting to cease their habit. Addictions are traditionally grouped according to what is believed to be the only or primary cause of a person's habit. For example, some addicts are said to have a "chemical addiction" to drugs or alcohol. A "physical addiction," however, could involve exercise—some people feel as though they "just have to run" on a regular basis. Similarly, a "psychological addiction" might involve some type of gambling, as when players feel compelled to spend many consecutive hours and even days betting in a gambling casino.

In recent years leading researchers at the Harvard Medical School Division on Addictions have advanced a more sophisticated way of understanding addictions that recognizes possible interplay between chemical, physical, and psychological factors that may contribute to addiction. Called a Syndrome Model of Addiction, this theory asserts that a person's risk for developing an addiction depends on a combination of:

1. personal vulnerabilities (e.g., genetics)
2. exposure to an object or activity (e.g., living environment, including behaviors of people in various surroundings)
3. experiences with the object or activity of addiction (e.g., enjoying use of drugs or playing Internet games).

Some addictions, such as running, can actually have healthy as well as harmful effects. This underscores the importance of considering the overall effects of particular behaviors that may become habitual. Various forms of addiction (i.e., chemical, physical, or psychological) are often interconnected through biochemical processes that take place in the brain and other organs of the body. For example, a person addicted to running experiences physical and emotional enjoyment activated through biochemically stimulated electrical processes in their brain while having their heart and lungs mix oxygen with blood to nourish muscles at work. Addiction, however, can drive a person to overdo it, resulting in physical damage, such as torn muscles, dehydration, unhealthy weight loss, and so on. As another example, a person addicted to online gaming may also suffer from a substance abuse addiction (e.g., from excessive caffeine, nicotine, other drugs, or alcohol). These two conditions can be inseparable, meaning they may be co-causal or one may be at least related to the onset or continuation of the other.

Think about the idea of spending hours online browsing the Web, or chatting online with friends, or playing an online game without realizing how much time has passed. On the surface this sounds normal and harmless. Indeed many, if not most, Internet users access the Net every day in complete enjoyment, with no lingering problems. However, excessively engulfing oneself in online games, surfing the Web, or partaking in other online activities at the expense of real-life obligations is problematic. In such cases a person can become consumed and even dependent on the software

Addiction develops from a combination of genetic, psychological, and physical factors. Those with Internet addiction will neglect their real-life responsibilities in favor of online gaming, social networking, or surfing the Web. *(Source: AP Photo/Will Kincaid)*

or hardware they use and the rewards these technologies provide. They may also become dependent on substances in order to maintain their alertness and overall energy in order to play games for excessive periods of time with minimal food, sleep, or need to use the bathroom.

People can become "addicted" to almost anything in life from which they derive pleasure. Some "addicts" are addicted to drinking alcohol, smoking or using tobacco, gambling, or viewing explicit sexual material. More and more people are realizing that they know someone who is, or has been, addicted to the Internet, computers, or computer gaming. They were addicted because they were preoccupied with the Internet or felt compelled to use it repeatedly for extended periods of time without regard to its harmful consequences.

IS INTERNET ADDICTION REAL?

Currently Internet addiction is not officially recognized by the American Psychological Association (APA) as a mental disorder. However, there is some discussion about whether it should be added to the *Diagnostic and Statistical Manual of Mental Disorders-V* (DSM-V), as the DSM-IV is being revised. The APA defines mental disorders in the DSM, which is like the "bible" for psychology. A work group is considering adding Internet addiction, possibly to be called "addiction-like behavioral disorders," based on emerging research about the problem. Another proposal is to include a new category of "non-substance behavioral addictions," which would initially only contain the single disorder of gambling addiction. Debate about this matter involves recognition that gambling and gaming occur independent of the Internet, that money may be betted in either online gambling or online gaming, and that large numbers of young people are known to experience problem gambling and then pathological gambling after learning to bet on games they play.[3]

Internet-related addictions are not always recognized because traditionally accepted addictions (e.g., to substances) are more easily diagnosed with the aid of drug testing. Dr. Jerald Block, a psychiatrist who specializes in treating Internet addiction, argued that Internet addiction is now being recognized in some countries as a major health problem consisting of excessive use, withdrawal, tolerance, and negative consequences (e.g., altercations, lying, and fatigue). Some experts think it should be officially categorized in the *Diagnostic and Statistical Manual of Mental Disorders-V* (DSM-V) as a new disorder of impulse control. This would allow Internet addiction to be consistently recognized by health care professionals in their treatment of people with such affliction. In advancing this view, Block points out that South Korea has reported one online game-related murder and at least 10 deaths from blood clots resulting from sitting down for extended periods in Internet cafés.[2] Thus, while Internet addiction is not currently officially recognized by the American Psychiatric Association (APA), increasing numbers of researchers, health care professionals, and policymakers throughout much of the connected world express increasing concern about the amount of time and consequences that people are experiencing from engaging online in seemingly unproductive ways that cause them and people in their lives to suffer.

INTERNET ADDICTION

While there may be no "official" definition of Internet addiction, Dictionary.com defines addiction as "the state of being enslaved to a habit or practice or to something that is psychologically or physically habit-forming, as narcotics, to such an extent that its cessation causes severe trauma." Therefore Internet addiction may be defined as being enslaved to the habit of using the Internet, so much so that giving it up would cause severe physical or psychological trauma. Internet addiction is associated with excessive use, feelings of frustration when unable to get online, and is connected to personal problems such as lack of success or relationship problems in real life. Yet one is not truly addicted to the Internet in and of itself but to certain kinds of content and/or activities it allows the user to experience. For example, one may be addicted to playing online games (common all over the world, especially in Korea), or may be addicted to social networking sites, chatting, and instant messaging, or to surfing Web sites in search of something new and exciting. It is not a true addiction, however, unless giving it up, or the thought of giving it up, causes adverse side effects. Therefore those addicted to the Internet have a hard time controlling the impulse to get online and seek out the content and/or activities that give them pleasure.

When most people think of a person being addicted, they commonly think of someone who smokes cigarettes, drinks too much alcohol, or is dependent on drugs such as cocaine or heroin. People become addicted to certain substances and/or activities for numerous reasons and once they become addicted, they lose control of themselves. It is also true that people can simultaneously experience more than one form of addiction, such as alcoholism, along with another addiction, such as online gambling or gaming. It is quite difficult to break an addiction, and even more difficult to break combinations of addiction.

So what about someone who might spend countless hours online, surfing the Web? Playing video games? Engaging in online shopping to the point where they are in serious credit card debt? All of these activities can be considered forms of addiction and can be quite harmful to the person committing the action and those who are related to them. Computing technology has provided people with expanded ways to communicate; yet it also has unleashed new ways to enjoy various forms of entertainment, including gaming, shopping, and meeting new people via various social networking sites. As a result, it is possible to become addicted to things that are made much easier through computing technology. Such behavior is common among teens and adults, and because IT devices are readily available along with various user-friendly social networking, gaming, and communication software, it is quite easy for one to become immersed in computing technology.

Young people have become more and more consumed with social networking sites, chatting, and online games. For some, these daily activities are quite important and not being able to partake in them can cause serious frustration and mental duress. Take for instance the episode of *Oprah* in which she invited a family to remove themselves from their IT devices for a short period of time and live off-line. They were encouraged to explore other activities that do not utilize laptops, gaming systems, and cell phones. The teenagers in the household had quite a hard time adapting to daily life without their cell phones and became quite temperamental about their inability to text and check social networking sites such as MySpace and Facebook. Indeed many young people would feel lost or disconnected if IT devices were removed from their daily routine for any length of time. For youth, the need to be connected is vital, and whether or not they are texting, it is important to have such devices ready and at their disposal if needed. Yet, does the idea that most young people would feel lost without their technology mean that they are addicted to it?

THE SOCIAL AND ECONOMIC HARMS AND IMPACT OF ADDICTIONS

Sadly, addictions such as alcoholism can yield both social and economic harms that can affect the addicted person and those around them. Friends, family, coworkers, and community members can be negatively affected financially, emotionally, and even physically by someone who is addicted. The nature and amount of harm experienced by the addict and other people in his or her life depends on the form and extent of the addiction. It is also true that many people afflicted with an addiction are thought of or accused of being morally deficient for choosing to experience or perhaps repeatedly engage in a vice of some kind. Consequently some people are labeled "an addict" in a mean-spirited way rather than in a compassionate way consistent with recognizing that people so afflicted require intervention, treatment, and support.

Those who know or are close to someone who is addicted are also affected by their addiction on a number of levels. Someone who is suffering from alcoholism can be a danger to themselves and those around them for numerous reasons. Indeed, Internet addiction in all its forms frequently involves consuming drugs and/or alcohol to stimulate or depress a user's physiology while increasing the pleasure of their online experiences. Thus the potential for incurring various short- and long-term health problems as a result of frequent intoxication or excessive reliance on Internet content or interactions can be deadly. A person's work can also be negatively affected because of their inability to perform in a proper manner or produce a quality product. Lastly, friendships and relationships can be affected based on the person's constant desire to sustain their habit(s) and whether or not their friends or family wish to engage in the activity with them or accept their behavior.

It is a common joke for many people to say that they know others (or maybe even themselves) who are addicted to social networking sites such as Facebook. The person might check their page many times throughout the day at work, school, and while on-the-go. The joke usually involves the idea that they cannot get off the social networking sites or that they are *always on.* Some might even feel the need to tweet about what they are doing or comment to their friends, using their mobile device before they get home from work or school. Friends or family may feel left out if someone is tweeting someone else while they are hanging out or working with the person who is sending the message. Addiction to a certain form of social computing content or activity, such as those offered by millions of Web pages and various online services, can also cause friends, family, or coworkers of an addict to feel left out when an addict they care deeply about forgoes relationships or responsibilities in favor of being online. Some might feel upset if a friend posts a status update and they are not included in the update. All of these actions represent the need for youth to stay connected, whether it is through social networking Web sites, texting, or instant messaging.

Furthermore, the need to stay connected can be quite harmful if it consumes the person who is addicted. For example, imagine how difficult it may be for someone who is addicted to texting, but they are at school. The school might ban cell phones or limit texting. Still, one might be able to get around such rules. By texting during school, one fails to listen to the teacher and fellow classmates, missing important material, which can affect future test performance and future class success as well as personal relationships with classmates. Getting caught texting during school could also lead to negative effects, such as the punishment of having the cell phone confiscated. People consumed in texting their friends and families have also engaged in the dangerous behavior of texting while driving. Many accidents, including the death of many

Modern technology has enabled people to remain constantly connected through the Internet. Texting with cell phones is a popular form of communication that can become a harmful addiction. *(Source: AP Photo/Aberdeen American News, Andrew Lamberson)*

young adults, can be blamed on texting or talking on the phone while driving.

In 2007, five girls from Fairport, New York, who were en route to a friend's home, were killed five days after their high school graduation when their SUV swerved into oncoming traffic and collided with a tractor-trailer. Bailey Goodman, the driver of the SUV, had received a text message shortly before the accident.[4] Similar to drinking and driving, the dangerous behavior of texting and driving can negatively impair a driver from paying attention to their surroundings and properly driving. This accident, in addition to many others, signified the need for legislation that would ban texting and driving. As of this writing, 30 states plus the District of Columbia now ban drivers using handheld devices.

ATTITUDES, BEHAVIORS, AND CHARACTERISTICS OF ONLINE ADDICTS

Many Internet users have a common urge to check the time and wonder when they will next be able to go online and play their favorite video game. It is also common for some to try to log into their favorite social networking Web sites during work or school, even though they are prohibited from doing so. The need to be "online" is a growing trend among youth. Young people enjoy staying "connected" and like to be available to communicate with their peers at anytime of day. Teens enjoy going to areas where they can use the Internet and their IT devices freely. Young adults increasingly prefer to travel only to places where there is a strong signal for a cell phone that allows for fast wireless connection to the Internet. People enjoy seeing HD televisions, Ethernet jacks, DVD players, and gaming consoles in their hotel rooms.

It is important to distinguish the difference between a person making heavy but reasonable use of an IT device for professional or personal purposes and a person becoming addicted to using an IT device that affects their personal and/or professional life. Certain traits or tendencies can be noted as similar to those in someone who is addicted to an illegal substance. For instance, a person who is addicted to a certain activity will compulsively engage in the activity even if he or she does not want to. Furthermore, if a person cannot engage in the activity, withdrawal symptoms such as craving, irritability, and restlessness will occur. When someone is addicted to a certain activity, they do not have control of themselves and get lost in such activity. For example, a gamer will lose track of the number of hours they have played a certain game or how much money they have spent on games or gaming devices. Lastly, a person who becomes addicted to an activity generally denies such addiction, even though others can see the negative effects that have occurred as a result.

On a more formal level, researchers from Taiwan have proposed a number of symptoms for their "Diagnostic Criteria for Internet Addiction for College Students." They asserted that six or more symptoms must be present for a diagnosis of Internet addiction. While it is unknown at this time whether the proposal will be accepted by the American Psychological Association (APA), the symptoms do describe many characteristics thought to be found in online addicts. Among those identified are excessive preoccupation, uncontrolled impulses and impairment of control, tolerance and withdrawal, and impaired decision making and function.[5] Other symptoms include using the Internet more than intended, and excessive time and effort devoted to the Internet. It is still not always clear, however, what the cutoff point is for those who are addicted and those who are not. Still, for those who are addicted, their "real" lives are substantially disrupted. For youth of today, this can mean spending most nonschool hours on a computer, doing worse in school, dropping out of "real-life" social groups, and feeling very angry when not able to use the computer.

CAUSES OF INTERNET ADDICTION

Addiction does not happen by accident and can occur based on interplay between chemical and biochemical processes along with psychological, emotional, and environmental factors that include objects and activities addicts use and how they regard these experiences (e.g., being pleasurable). This means that people can be more susceptible to becoming addicted based on their family history, the things they do, and their ability to tolerate stress or resist impulses. Understanding possible causes of Internet addiction is important so that we can assist those who are troubled by this.

Chemical and Biological Causes

Chemical addiction is the result of ingesting a substance that contains addictive materials affecting the body to a point which causes a person to desire more of the substance on a more frequent basis. For example, someone who starts to smoke cigarettes is inhaling nicotine, which is a powerful, addictive drug. Once nicotine enters the bloodstream, the body craves more and more of it, and as a result causes a smoker to feel out of control when not smoking on a regular basis. Generally, chemical addiction is the result of the abuse of the substance. Addicts cannot function properly unless they consume the substance, and withdrawal can be very difficult and even fatal in some cases.

The disease model of addiction is based on activities of the brain. More specifically, it involves the area of the brain that activates the release of a chemical called dopamine. When dopamine binds to receptors in the forebrain area of the brain, it causes feelings of pleasure. Dopamine is responsible for many human functions such as movement, attention, and the ability to experience excitement and pleasure. Addictive substances, like nicotine, cause a false stimulation because they bind to the dopamine receptors. As a result, more dopamine remains and causes pleasurable feelings for longer periods of time. It is believed that certain stronger drugs such as cocaine cause the release of much higher levels of dopamine than activities such as eating or drinking, and therefore they are considered much more addictive. For addicts, drugs (and/or other things) become a substitute for normal activities that cause pleasure, meaning that drugs are *needed* to achieve pleasure. Desires and cravings can become so strong it is very difficult for an addict's body to give up the object of addiction. In effect, the brain "learns" that it needs the substance to achieve the reward.

Cigarette companies use this to their advantage. They have also actively sought new ways to use computing technologies to market their product and appeal to more consumers and create new forms of products. In 2003, an electronic cigarette or personal vaporizer was introduced that offered a user a way to inhale doses of nicotine via a vaporized solution out of a battery-powered device. This gave companies a new product to market that also included new flavors not normally available in regular cigarettes. Once a user purchased the main tube that holds the nicotine liquid, they would only need to purchase refills for the tube, which in turn offered a cost-saving option. While this new form of smoking provided a new sensation to its users, it still made users of the product addicted after ingesting the nicotine on a regular basis. These electronic cigarettes are also controversial because the health risks have yet to be determined. They are banned in some countries due to safety concerns.

Biological causes of addiction may include behavior that is already "programmed in" as a result of family traits that have been passed down over time. An example of a hereditary cause of addiction would include a family member who is more susceptible to drinking alcohol based on other family members having been diagnosed with alcoholism. However, not all children of alcoholics, or children of parents who suffer from other forms of addiction, are destined to become addicts themselves. Rather, children of addicts may be at greater risk of acquiring the same or another form of addiction caused by genetics or other factors that combine in ways that are hard to understand. In recent years medical professionals have advanced a Syndrome Model of Addiction to help explain complicated ways in which physical and environmental circumstances may combine with an individual's consumption of drugs and/or alcohol to affect biochemical processes in the brain that further affect psychological responses, decision making, and behaviors.[6] Thus determining what precisely causes or merely contributes to the onset and continuing state of addiction among individuals varies greatly and is often difficult, even for trained medical professionals, to diagnose and treat effectively.

BRAIN ACTIVITIES AND GAMING ADDICTION

In an article published in the *Journal of Psychiatric Research*, a number of scientists from Taiwan discussed their research that compared brain activities in people who had been diagnosed with an addiction to online gaming addiction.[7] Their study noted that there has not been much research done on brain activities (neural mechanisms) for those addicted to online gaming. In other words they explored whether areas of the brain that are associated with the strong desire to play were more activated for people who are addicted to gaming. Using functional magnetic resonance imaging (MRI technology that shows a dynamic image of areas of the brain working), the study showed that specific areas of the brains of gaming addicts were activated when they were shown pictures of gaming (as opposed to another group that was shown mosaic pictures). The researchers found that brain-activation patterns among online gaming addicts were very similar to the brain-activation patterns of people with substance addiction. This shows that certain behavioral addictions, such as to online gaming or the Internet, may be more like addictions to substances than previously thought. Perhaps this research will be used by those arguing to include Internet and gaming addiction in the DSM-V.

Another cutting-edge study using functional MRI was conducted by researchers at the Stanford University School of Medicine. These researchers also explored brain activity during gaming, but they focused on whether the activities were different for men than for women. They found that study participants showed activity in the mesocorticolimbic center of the brain, which is the area of the brain associated with reward and addiction. The activity levels were much higher in the males, however, than they were for females in the study game, which had a goal of gaining more space and territory. From this, the researchers believed that the neural circuitry in the male brain tends to make males more likely to be addicted to computer games, especially those with goals of obtaining territory or which involve aggression.[8] More research is needed to clarify this.

Psychological, Emotional, and Environmental Causes

Psychological causes of addiction can be described as the ways that people relate to the behavior in which they partake. If a certain behavior makes them feel better, they are more likely to take part in it. This could even involve playing a sport or exercising, which often results in feelings of exhilaration afterward. A significant amount of energy is exerted during a sporting event, and the body releases certain chemicals that make one feel good about the activity. Such chemicals are called endorphins. In some cases people live for these feelings and enjoy the psychological joy they feel from activities that produce them. Furthermore, good feelings associated with past events can contribute to the desire to perform the same activity again. Even distant memories can contribute to our decision making for future events. Feeling good about participating in a certain activity because of positive feelings makes one more likely to take part in that behavior in the future.

People may also become addicted because they are compensating for the feeling that something is missing in their lives. In short, they may feel unfulfilled or have a low opinion of themselves, and therefore turn to some form of external support. While this support could be something positive like more time spent with family or friends or commitment to a healthy lifestyle, it could also be something negative like excessive use of drugs, gambling, or using the Internet. These "supports" cause people to feel better, at least in the short term, because it relieves their sense of anxiety and offers a form of self-medication. This leads to an addiction when they become dependent on their support in order to cope with life. Sometimes, when they realize they need the support, they become even unhappier, which leads to a destructive cycle of addiction.

Environmental causes of addiction can be easier to understand by realizing that one can become addicted to a certain behavior based on similar behaviors of people with whom they interact. Young people who grow up in a household that enjoys eating sugary snacks and unhealthy food are more likely to make and serve such food when they run a household of their own. This is because they became accustomed to eating or acting in a certain way based on behaviors of people who surrounded them while growing up.

Other environmental factors such as drinking intoxicating beverages and/or excessive online gaming by family members or friends may also contribute to a person's Internet addiction.

CONCLUSION

Addiction is a condition in which a person is physically and/or psychologically dependent on a substance or activity to such an extent they experience trauma in their lives as a result of their behavior or as a consequence of attempting to cease their habit. Addiction is often misunderstood for several reasons. For example, the onset of addiction and how much of something is excessive varies widely among people, as does the amount of harm associated with quitting or not quitting a habit. In addition, being "addicted" to something is a medical condition, but it is often construed as someone having a moral problem. When this occurs, victims of a health problem may suffer even more from being labeled an "addict."

Addiction can also be confusing because so many things typically lead to or result from an addiction. Dr. Howard Shafer of the Harvard Medical School Division on Addictions refers to many habit-forming things that work in combination as the Syndrome Model of Addiction. This powerful concept means that many things may contribute to so-called Internet addiction, as when a person is addicted to alcohol and online gaming. In contrast, excessive gambling and overeating were not really considered addictive until determined to be disorders of impulse control by medical professionals. Now Internet addiction, online gaming and gambling, and even eating disorders connected with excessive Web activity are increasingly recognized and accepted as conditions that warrant attention, prevention, intervention, or treatment.

Social Computing and Online Addictions

In February 2008, a 15-year-old boy named Hughstan Schlicker called 911 and informed the dispatcher that he had shot and killed his father with a shotgun. Schlicker later told police that his father had taken away his access to the Internet because his father had found Hughstan's suicide threats that he had posted on MySpace. Then, after calling in sick to school (pretending to be his father), he found his father's shotgun in the garage. He took the gun to his room with the intention of killing himself in front of his father, but he changed his plan and decided to kill his father first, and then himself. When his father came home early at 2 p.m., he walked up behind him in the kitchen and shot him in the back of the head.

As to the reason why, Schlicker, who would spend full days on MySpace, said he could not accept the thought of not being able to access the social networking site. According to Schlicker, losing access to MySpace "…felt like I was stabbed with a knife and it went straight through and…no matter how hard I pulled, I couldn't pull out the knife." Schlicker was indicted on charges of first degree murder, and in 2009, he agreed to plead guilty to second degree murder as part of a deal for a lesser sentence. He was later sentenced to 20 years in prison.[1] It is unknown whether this teen had mental health issues other than just being addicted to MySpace and being angry over not being able to use it. During the court case, however, Schlicker was described as suicidal and angry at the time of the murder. Still, the incident shows how strong the emotional reaction was for one boy who was cut off from his online social world.

Boys and girls of today grow up surrounded by computing technology, and they have never known a world without the Internet. They use computers, cell phones, gaming devices, and other computing technologies to stay in touch with friends and family, solve problems, and be creative. On the other hand, adults or those people born prior to 1993 have experienced a world without the Internet. By growing up in a world without the Internet, adults have had to learn later in life how to use computing technology in the workplace and home. This is challenging for some adults as many consider the Internet and the growth of computing to be a nuisance or something that is difficult to use. In 2001, Mark Prensky, a designer of educational and training games, coined the concept of digital youth culture by distinguishing youth and adults as digital natives and digital immigrants. "Digital natives" are youth, or those who grew up with the technology, and adults, or "digital immigrants," are those adapting their lives to include computing technologies.[2] Still, adults are becoming more and more technologically savvy and are increasingly using social networking sites and embracing digital culture. Youth of today, however, live and breathe digital culture, so there is a gap that exists between them and adults.

To understand digital youth culture, one must understand the concept of culture. The term *culture* encompasses a person's or group's values, belief systems, and language. It is influenced by ecological, political, economic, and technological conditions. Cultures can coexist and commingle and share traditions and customs. For example, some families might have a certain tradition that they celebrate. Buying a Christmas tree the day after Thanksgiving, visiting grandparents during a certain holiday break, or sharing a special meal with family or friends on Sunday all represent traditions. Traditions vary based on the economic, political, and geographical environment. One who lives in the Northeast may share a family tradition of going skiing or enjoying the winter snowfall in early November, whereas in warmer climates another family may share a tradition such as boating during the holidays.

Digital youth culture shares common beliefs and values and even has its own language. To begin, digital youth culture encompasses the value that being online is normal and expected in computing societies. Youth love IT devices and the Internet and enjoy connecting from both public and private places. Kids enjoy learning from their peers and computing is substantially group- or self-taught with minimal training from adults. Furthermore, as a culture, youth enjoy being creative and competing to solve problems. To do this, youth engage in rapid-fire messaging by instant messaging or texting. Youth enjoy "showing off" their devices and expect their peers to have the "latest and greatest" forms of technology so that they can stay connected. It is common for youth to enjoy upgrading and sharing their new IT devices.

Language is an important aspect of culture and allows for people to share ideas, traditions, and history. Within digital youth culture, youth use "Leetspeak" to communicate with their peers. Leetspeak is a digital language that accelerates and disguises the meaning of communication. "Leet," also known as "l33t," is derived from the term *elite*, which shows a superior status. Leetspeak is used for the rapid-fire messaging because its shorthand method of communication is fast and provides privacy. Instead of typing out full sentences with proper punctuation, youth send short, coded messages to their peers. In some cases youth use l33t to hide the meaning of messages from parents who might be in the same room as them. Using terms such as POS, or "parent over shoulder," can easily alert peers that a parent is watching and to either wait to continue the conversation or refrain from a certain topic of discussion. In most cases, when parents see such communication, it is

Young people who grew up with the Internet and modern technology have become increasingly dependent on computers and cell phones. This has led to the development of a digital youth culture, with both negative and positive results. *(Source: Marco Prosch/Getty Images)*

hard for them to decipher or even begin to understand their child's communication.

Digital youth culture includes the need for constant communication and the ability for a peer to be available at any one moment. It is expected for youth to quickly fire back a response if they are texted or instant messaged (IMed). Instant messages, comment approvals, e-mails, and gaming forums are an important aspect of a child's online activity. Young people engage in rapid-fire messaging to numerous friends about various topics, including what happened in school, a current crush, or a current problem they are facing. With the increase in availability of data plans for cell phones, more young people are engaging in texting, which allows for instant exchange and relaying of messages. They enjoy communicating to their peers using texting and instant messaging and see no issue in using such communication while at work or school. Some even prefer to text each other rather than simply talk, even when in very close proximity to one another.

Their world view requires them to be constantly connected to the world and constantly connected to and available to their peers. Kids increasingly begin to use IT devices at earlier ages in life. Consider these findings from Rochester Institute of Technology's (RIT) 2007–2008 Survey of Internet and At-Risk Behaviors of K–12th grade students: [3]

- Of the 63 percent of 4,459 kindergarten and first-grade students surveyed in 2007–2008 use a home computer to access the Internet, 92 percent use their home computer to play electronic games, 66 percent watch videos or listen to music, 48 percent read or write e-mail, 41 percent talk with people on a Web site, and 49 percent look at Web sites for schoolwork.
- The study also found that as children age they use more types of devices to access the Internet. From the same RIT study it was learned that among 5,529 second- to third-grade students surveyed, 96 percent use a home computer to access the Internet, 23 percent use a portable video game console, 21 percent use a video game console, and 14 percent use a cell phone for the same kinds of things as younger children.

By the beginning of the fourth grade most kids in urban, suburban, and rural school settings also participate in numerous forms of online learning, entertainment, and social computing. RIT's research reveals that among 9,350 fourth- to sixth-graders surveyed in 2007–2008 about their Internet activities, 92 percent reported they play electronic games, 87 percent visit Web sites designed for kids, 80 percent listen to music, 72 percent watch videos or do schoolwork online, 54 percent read or write e-mail, 38 percent instant message, 26% participate in chat rooms, and

24% text message. Having grown up using computerized devices, and never having known a world without the constant connection and availability these devices provide, young people eagerly learn new IT skills and assume their place as members of worldwide digital youth culture. They also learn that they can create content in this world in any number of ways to creatively express themselves, while at the same time they can tailor their Internet experience to themselves. Youth of today are multitaskers who are adept at using the technology to choose what is entertaining for them. The RIT data clearly shows that this is happening at a very young age.

The use of technology by adults has also dramatically changed with technological improvements to the Internet and IT devices. In 2000, when the use of Wi-Fi was uncommon, about 46 percent of adults used the Internet, 5 percent had a broadband connection at home, 50 percent owned a cell phone, and none were able to connect to the Internet wirelessly.[4] In 2010, however, 75 percent of adults used the Internet, 62 percent had broadband at home, 80 percent had a cell phone, and 53 percent were able to connect to the Internet via wireless network. What is also changing, however, is the way in which adults are using technology as a means of social computing. For example, adults are increasingly using computers for social networking purposes (contrary to a belief that these sites are only for youth). So while social networking does remain more popular among teens than adults, more than one-third of adult Internet users in 2010 had a profile on a social networking site, a quadrupling of such users in just four years. This popularity can be misleading, however, because one-third of U.S. adults comprise a much larger group of people than the 65 percent of U.S. teens who use social networking sites. Otherwise stated, more adults, albeit younger adults especially between the ages of 18 and 24, use social networking sites than teens.[5] Worldwide it is also true that kids born after the onset of the World Wide Web, in 1993, are now becoming adults and soon will be having children of their own, thereby introducing another new generation of Internet users.

ALARMING ASPECTS OF INTERNET AND DIGITAL YOUTH CULTURE

Unfortunately, with digital communication among youths, online incivility, promiscuity, abuse, and crime are also common. This behavior is often expected and tolerated by young people. Sending and receiving mean or nasty messages is done routinely by many— though not all—youth. Also, for many young people, discussion of sexually explicit content or malicious conversation is quite common via text or instant message. The specter of "sexting" is also common as underage kids exchange sexually suggestive and even naked photos of themselves online. Many underage users also lie about their age, appearance, and other personal matters when communicating with friends through instant messaging or Web profiles. For many youth, online incivility is not something that is necessarily bad, but is rather accepted by their peers.

Research suggests that increasing numbers of youth engage in some type of cyberabuse or offending after learning to do so from their peers. A negative aspect of viral information sharing includes overcoming blocking or filtering software. Students enrolled in school laptop programs across the country typically encounter blocked Web sites while they are learning in the classroom. However, some youth are able to find out ways around software filters and blocks. Once this is done, the information is commonly shared, enabling everyone to access restricted sites. This is similar to when rumors and gossip are quickly spread through social networking sites, texting, and instant messaging as a way of inciting or promulgating cyberbullying. Messages that are spread quickly and virally online can cause much greater harm than face-to-face communication, though these often occur simultaneously. It is important to remember that the Internet never forgets. Many young people enjoy posting digital content that might include inappropriate material, such as a nude photograph. Major portions of the Internet are recorded daily by some governments, and users anywhere can also save content that is discovered or shared. So even if the person who created and/or posted a picture or video removed it from their own device(s) and Web profile, it will likely always be available to authorities or other people who already saved the image to their computer. Firms like Google and Facebook own content posted to the Web sites they host, which means that considerable amounts of social networking content long-since removed by users remains archived. Users everywhere beware—never post or send anything online that you might regret later in life. What happens online stays online.

According to the RIT study, Survey of Internet and At-Risk Behaviors, young people begin to use computers and other IT devices at a very young age. Kids surveyed in that study revealed they first become mean to other people online when they are in second grade. Also according to this study, use of computers or other IT devices, and the range of purposes for which these are used, also increases with age. For example, pirating of music, movies, and software begins as early as fourth grade. The RIT study also revealed that beginning in the fourth grade there are more adolescent offenders than victims. By middle school, students as a group engage in all known forms of online abuse and crime except corporate espionage and so-called cyberterrorism. Victims of cyberabuse and cybercrime generally know who the offenders are; often they are friends or classmates. As a result, more time and activities online generally equate to more offending and victimization.

POSITIVE ATTITUDES AND YOUTH BEHAVIORS ONLINE

Digital youth culture has many positive aspects and nearly all the young people who make up digital youth culture are *not* troubled or otherwise deviant. Youth use the Internet to engage in teaming and problem solving, and they enjoy supporting each other with their technological devices. It is important for young friends to stay in touch with each other by IMing, texting, or posting messages on social networking sites such as MySpace or Facebook. Boys and girls also enjoy using the Net to search for information that might assist them with their homework or daily life. They use the Web to learn new information and to research information about colleges, politics, and other areas of interest. Sharing information is important, and once a piece of information is found out, it is shared "virally" to others using cell phones, instant messaging, or Web blogs.

Students enjoy it when classes include IT devices to learn new subjects or engage in group projects. Many schools across the United States have added Internet-ready computers to classrooms and offered laptop programs for elementary through high school students. This allows youth to easily engage in teaming and problem solving while using Internet search engines to find information. Upon the request of a teacher or professor, students can retrieve and share information instantly, in and outside of classrooms. In ways consistent with digital youth culture, connected students are learning to team up online to quickly solve problems in innovative ways. Active learning through online interactions is exciting for students and teachers as they discover new ways in which to use IT devices to access Web content and share information critical to effective problem solving. In ad hoc ways people everywhere are learning faster and more creatively than ever.

SOCIAL COMPUTING

Information technologies have changed how people communicate and interact for all sorts of things. Nowhere are changes more evident than in behaviors, attitudes, and feelings expressed by users who engage in social computing. Also known as "social networking," social computing involves all the ways in which people socialize online. Online socialization occurs via e-mail, IM, text, Twitter, various personal profile Web sites such as Facebook, online games, and even YouTube.

It is important to understand that social computing is not merely a set of potentially interrelated online activities involving chat. Rather, social computing is an incredible human force enabled by technology. Innovative learning among teachers and students now occurs via social computing. But learning through social computing is not limited to classrooms in schools. Kids and adults now use IT devices and the Net to create various types of documents not related to schoolwork. They also shop, listen to music, watch movies, and play electronic games. They do these and many other things alone or with friends, while online or off-line, with decreasing concerns about being in relatively close proximity to each other or separated by great distances. All this is made possible by the Net, Web content, and portable IT devices, especially smart phones. For millions of users throughout the world social computing and mobile computing are now inseparable concepts that seemingly enable them to do almost anything possible online while on the go. As more users engage in social-mobile computing, the very nature of society stands to change. For example, in 2011, the Egyptian government was reformed partly because of mass protests in Cairo and other cities organized through social computing by mobile users.

Incredibly, the social computing site Facebook now gets more hits than Google on a given day. This is because Internet resources such as Facebook, Yahoo!, and YouTube inspire and enable sharing of information while providing quick, efficient, and enjoyable ways for people to socialize. The amazing ability of technology to allow people to connect is the secret to its success. Likewise, online gaming as an important form of social computing is sensationally successful because of the *people factor*. Thus social computing facilitates a basic human need for interaction, to feel close and included, and to relate to others in far-reaching ways.

Young people especially enjoy communicating with online friends while using their personal computer, cell phone, or gaming console. The Internet provides borderless communication in which kids can interact with other kids in a different town, state, or even country. Social computing sites such as MySpace, Yahoo!, or Facebook allow easy searching for people in different areas of the world who share similar interests. Use of social computing Web sites may require creating an online profile, which usually includes a picture and personal information pertaining to interests, school, employment, and marital status. Regardless of how social computing sites are used, the main purpose of creating personal profiles is to build a network of online friends in order to post, view, and share content.

ADDICTIVE ASPECTS OF SOCIAL COMPUTING

When asked about their online activities, kids frequently indicate they have dozens if not hundreds or even thousands of online friends. They enthusiastically describe what they find interesting and like to do online, which usually involves social computing sometimes for hours and hours without interruption. Whether a user's social computing involves chat for chat's sake, or puzzle solving to learn new things, or competing with hundreds of gamers playing a massively multiplayer online role-playing game (MMORPG), *they* obviously feel the activity is worthwhile or else they would not voluntarily engage in it. Like any other kind of human endeavor, however, too much of a good thing can be unhealthy. Overeating and overexercising are not good. Neither is excessive social computing. Unfortunately, the simple and sad truth is that some users obsess about being online, whether to view particular forms of content or to engage in certain kinds of social computing that incorporates alluring things into online exchanges. Viewing pornography or engaging in sex-related chat online are obvious examples of online activities that can be very alluring to some users. Sexting among teens is a kind of social computing brought on perhaps by curiosity and desires to be erotic with friends. Social computing as a form or aspect of Internet addiction, however, does not necessarily involve sex-related content or communications. Any form of stimulating content may be communicated, and therefore many forms of social computing may become addictive for some users, especially when combined with substance abuse. Continuously feeling as though they need to view or otherwise connect with certain kinds of content or online friends, users susceptible to social computing, *as a factor in a syndrome of addiction,* may feel angst, become upset, and even experience withdrawal symptoms like depression when denied access to the Net.

The increasingly interactive and dynamic nature of the Internet makes it very appealing to people who are seeking connections. Therefore more and more people are connected to, communicating with, and forming relationships with others online. In fact many people go online because they are seeking relationships, or

DOES WEB 3.0 TECHNOLOGY "PUSH" ADDICTION?

Trends and advancements in technology are reshaping how people use the Web. Continuous access on multiple devices has ushered in the next generation of the Internet: Web 3.0. Conceivably, the potential of Web 3.0, which is intended to stimulate and enable individualized Internet-centric lifestyles, has implications for Internet addiction. Consider the following:

Many people now subscribe to one or more Internet TV-movie viewing services. Like many kinds of businesses that market and sell things online, the firm uses Web 3.0 technology to cleverly advertise things in personal ways to its customers. How does this happen? When customers first sign up for the service they (probably) complete a short survey about what they enjoy watching. This enables the service provider to customize an entire set of viewing suggestions that are then used to prompt customers into making particular selections. Each time a customer views another movie they are asked to rate it. Later, while searching the service provider's Web site for more movies and programs to watch, customers automatically receive suggestions for viewing based on their survey data, individual ordering history, and prior and ongoing browsing activity. As this process continues over extended periods of time, customers' viewing preferences become better understood. This in turn allows "pop-up" viewing suggestions along with advertisements customized to the online shopping interests of customers. It also allows advertisements to be created and automatically programmed to appear on targeted viewing screens. In effect, customized Web sites are "pushed" to the attention of customers using Web 3.0 technology. It follows that a person who feels compelled to watch certain genres of Internet TV or movies could be served up irresistible types and amounts of alluring things to view, thereby supplying them content that fuels their Internet addiction.

wish to become affiliated with groups or clubs of some kind. This likely satisfies a basic human need to interact and share with others and possibly develop a deeper sense of intimacy or closeness with them. The Internet provides many ways to form relationships because it offers a way to instantly connect with so many people. Yet, despite common interests that people share or may develop, relationships that are formed only online may differ significantly from face-to-face relationships in positive and negative ways. For some, the need to stay connected becomes too strong, and they have a difficult time staying away from this. They become preoccupied with getting onto the sites and seeing what is going on, as with a popular social networking feature that enables people to share what they are doing or thinking in the moment. Therefore it can become a form of compulsion that involves wanting to get away from the real world and spending more time in the digital

THE ADDICTED NURSE

Maria Garcia is a nurse who says she always fulfills her responsibilities on the job. This is the case even though she only gets about three hours of sleep per day. The reason she is so sleep deprived? She states this is because of the social networking site Facebook. According to Garcia, she goes to sleep at around 3 A.M. and gets up a few hours later to begin her day with about four hours of Facebook! Then she is off to work, only to return in the evening for three or four more hours of Facebooking. Add the total hours of Facebook during an average week for Garcia and it amounts to a staggering 56 hours—16 more than a full-time workweek. She states, "Everybody at work is talking about Facebook and it seemed really interesting, a way to socialize with my friends. But then, little by little, I got into all the games that are going on and just got addicted to it." When asked about giving up Facebook for one week, she exclaimed, "I would freak out."[6]

INTERNET ADDICTION AND ONLINE GAMING

world. The most observable signs of a problem are when a user enjoys spending more time in the digital world than the real world. When this happens, excessive time may be spent online, causing relationships, work, and personal health to suffer.

There is also an addictive social component to online gaming as friendships are developed with other players. Many games require collaboration among players to achieve success, which requires extensive investments of *time*. There also may be online peer pressure involved, which encourages players to keep playing, and keep playing hard, to achieve team success. This may contribute to addictive tendencies of a player because they do not want leave to the game and face the social consequences.

CONCLUSION

Technological advancements since creation of the Internet and emergence of the World Wide Web are astounding. Information technology has dramatically transformed how people communicate, socialize, research, shop, learn, work, share, teach, play, and are otherwise entertained. Yet the ways in which people interact online are also astounding and have everything to do with IT-enabled communication. In short, the Net, computers and other types of IT devices have forever *changed* the way people communicate and interact.

Changes are observable in the behaviors, attitudes, and feelings of technology users. Small wonder that social networking sites, such as Facebook, now surpass Google with the number of Internet hits received every day. For people, young and old, going online is a leading form of entertainment and also part of Internet and digital youth culture as well as social computing. Whether playing, seeking mental stimulation, or looking for an escape from the real world, going online is also a way to interact and connect with people. Electronic gaming often involves social interactions, which is a key reason people play games in the first place. Perhaps it is the interaction with *people* along with playing games that is addictive. After all, among millions of Internet users, relatively few are addicted to gaming or anything else for that matter. Still, there is particular fascination and uncertainty about connections between any form of social computing and addiction.

Online Gaming and
Addiction

*When thinking about online gaming, the idea of someone being
harmed is usually not the first thing to come to mind. However,
consider the case of a Korean couple who, in March 2010, were
arrested for allegedly neglecting their three-month-old daughter
who died of malnutrition. The couple reportedly spent all night at a
PC bang, a popular type of online gaming club in South Korea, and
upon returning home, they found her dead.[1] They also allegedly
admitted to spanking her often, feeding her rotten powdered milk,
and often leaving her at home alone while they attended extended
gaming sessions at clubs. In August 2010, in another extreme case, a
man collapsed and died after playing games for more than 50 hours
straight at a PC bang. In a May 2009 case, a 12-year-old boy living
in Bangkok committed suicide by leaping off a sixth-floor veranda
at his school. An investigation into the case revealed that the parents
had taken away his video games because they thought he was playing them too much. In response, the boy sent messages through his
cell phone to his parents and friends, stating that "tomorrow is my*

last day."[2] While these examples are extreme cases resulting in tragic outcomes, addiction cases pertaining to online gaming are generally not "extreme" at all. They can, however, result in real harm to individuals. These examples demonstrate the need for parents, educators, and youth to discuss dangerous aspects of online gaming and the need to regulate behavior. Before examining negative aspects of online gaming and addiction, an overview of the phenomenon of online and electronic gaming will be explored.

The growth of online and electronic (off-line) gaming has allowed people to engage in various types of play from assorted locations day and night. Until the invention of digital games, gaming consisted mostly of playing cards or board games in homes or parlors, or playing pinball machines that were typically located in arcades. In 1962, this all changed with the introduction of *Spacewar!,* which was an early and popular digital game. In the decades that followed, as computers became more powerful, more affordable, and smaller, the number and variety of electronic games that could be played on them increased exponentially.

Today users can choose between thousands of different game titles within many different categories of games known as genres (e.g., first-person shooter games). And with available desktop and laptop computers, gaming consoles, portable gaming devices, and cell phones that also enable playing electronic games while on the go, users now have a seemingly infinite number of games and playing circumstances to choose from and enjoy. People around the world now engage in various forms of gaming, using all sorts of IT devices. Indeed people now play games with others who need not be in the same room or building, or even in the same country. Gamers commonly purchase a gaming device such as PlayStation or the latest Xbox, along with appealing gaming software. Gamers can purchase gaming hardware and software in stores, from Web sites of online retailers, or they can download free games from various Web sites. In relatively short periods of time many gamers assemble large collections of games. Families with children of different ages or with members who enjoy gaming together may own a wide variety of games. Some Web browser service sites also provide games for Internet users. For example, Yahoo! offers e-mail, calendaring, a search engine, social computing, and a variety of games for users to explore and play.

Although games can be found in many places online, it is important to understand that pirating games is illegal. Violators of copyright laws around the world now face criminal prosecution and costly civil lawsuits brought on by game developers, manufacturers, and distributors. For this reason gamers must ensure that the games they play were paid for and that they are legally authorized to use them.

Hardware capabilities that can support video streaming and other data-intensive computing operations are essential for enjoying modern computer games. Users must ensure they have satisfactory graphics cards, joysticks, and random access memory (RAM) required by games they intend to play. Although most gamers happily settle for commercially available games, some people enjoy programming their own electronic games or designing and building custom gaming systems. Some schools now have electronic gaming clubs for students, and a few universities now offer college courses and even complete degrees in computer gaming. Students who pursue computer gaming studies are increasingly finding employment opportunities in this broadening and lucrative professional field.

With advances in computer technology, several different genres of electronic games have emerged. For example, racing games, sports games, and fighting games are three different genres of electronic games that imitate these kinds of real-world activities. Racing games involve different forms of racing like motocross or car racing. Examples include *Shift 2 Unleashed: Need for Speed, Dirt 2*, and *NASCAR*. Sports games imitate popular and professional sports such as hockey, football, baseball, basketball, soccer, and golf.

Fighting games typically feature digital characters hand-fighting with or without weapons of some kind. Examples include *Street Fighter IV, Mortal Kombat, Tekken,* and *UFC Undisputed.* Similarly, first-person shooter (FPS) games, such as *Call of Duty: Modern Warfare series,* typically involve a player assuming the role of a protagonist

Players line up to meet the developers of *World of Warcraft* at the launch for a new version of the game. Massive multiplayer online role-playing games allow people to interact with other users from around the world in the game. *(Source: Casey Rodgers/AP Images for Blizzard)*

avatar in a hostile environment that consists of threats to be targeted and fired upon with one or more types of weapons.

Another significant category is massive multiplayer online role-playing games (MMORPGs), which involve thousands of users playing simultaneously. Popular examples include *World of Warcraft*, *Guild Wars,* and *Final Fantasy XIV.* Sometimes also called "MMOGs" (massive multiplayer online games), these games stress character interactions and teaming to solve puzzles or complete "quests" for experience or other power-up items. Action-adventure games like *Grand Theft Auto IV, Mafia II,* and *Magicka: Vietnam* involve players assuming an avatar role to explore, discover, and accomplish "missions" of some sort. These games tend to be puzzle-based investigations or include interactions with other characters-players. These games are heavily reliant on story lines and draw inspiration from history, movies, television, literature, and other media.

Casual games are usually associated with traditional off-line board games, card games, puzzle games, or word games. Digital examples include *Monopoly 3*, *Solitaire*, *World of Goo*, *Diner Dash 2*, *Bejeweled 2 Deluxe*, and *Tetris*. Rhythm games generally involve simulating the playing of a musical instrument such as guitar, playing in a band, dancing, or being a disc jockey. One of the most famous rhythm games is *Guitar Hero*, which involves playing a plastic guitar and fretting the "notes" and "strumming" along while keeping in time with all types of recorded songs. Similar and more recent versions of this popular game series include *Rock Band 3*, *Guitar Hero III: Legends of Rock*, *Guitar Hero: Aerosmith*, and *Guitar Hero: World Tour*. Simulation games place gamers in decision-making situations that depict real-life or make-believe experiences. For example, *Farming Simulator 2011* challenges players to assume the role of a farmer in growing crops and breeding animals. Similarly in *Flight Simulator 2010*, players act as pilots inside a cockpit to take off and land aircraft. And *Cities in Motion* has players create a perfect transportation system.

Other categories of electronic games aim to provide enjoyment while increasing players' skills along with their knowledge of things that sometimes extend beyond the game itself. In some cases, games are designed to promote certain kinds of toys or other products. *Barbie Fashion Show: An Eye for Style*, as its name implies, promotes Barbie doll toys and related products while also showcasing attractive styles of clothing. It is not surprising that many electronic games are designed to allure young people in some way and for all sorts of reasons. *Americas Army 3*, for example, is designed to be fun and attract young men and women to explore life as a soldier in the U.S. Army.

Gamers of all ages, including parents, members of interest groups, and kids themselves, are concerned about the nature and intensity of gaming content, especially if it involves violence or sex. The Entertainment Software Rating Board (ESRB) assigns rating symbols to all kinds of videos, including electronic games. A total

YOUTH, ADULTS, AND GAMING

Nearly all teenage boys (99 percent) and teenage girls (94 percent) play video games. The age group considered most likely to play video games, however, is younger teens between the ages of 12 and 14.[3] Similarly, as electronic gaming devices have become more advanced and mobile, smaller handheld devices are also more likely to be played by younger teens. Specifically, 60 percent of teens use portable devices (PlayStation PSP or Nintendo DS, etc.) for gaming, but more teens ages 12 to 14 use them as opposed to older teens aged 15 to 17. Younger teens are also more likely than older teens to play online games, and they are also more likely to play certain types of games. For example, teens between the ages of 12 and 14 are more likely to play sports and adventure games than older teens, and are more likely to explore virtual worlds such as *Second Life* or *Club Penguin*.[4]

Gaming is not an activity exclusively for teens and kids. Research also indicates that more than one-half of adults over the age of 18 (53 percent) play video games, with about one in five playing every day.[5] Yet, as adults age, they are less likely to play video games. For example, while more than 8 out of 10 adults age 18 to 29 play video games, only 1 out of 5 adults over the age of 65 do the same. About 60 percent of adults between the ages of 30 and 49 play video games, as compared to only 40 percent of adults between the ages of 50 and 64. Adults, different than teens, prefer playing games on the computer, followed by on a console, cell phone, or portable device. Adult parents are more likely than adult nonparents to play electronic games using all types

of seven different rating symbols indicate a range of content a game contains and suggests appropriate viewing and playing ages. For example, the symbol "EC" stands for "Early Childhood" and means that a game labeled in this way has content that may be suitable for people three years or older. Similarly "[game] titles rated E10+

of devices. Parents can find it very hard to resist a child's familiar question, "Will you play with me?" Younger parents, however, are more inclined to say yes to this question than older parents. Still, while adults are more likely to use a computer to play games, they are less likely than teens to play games online. Overall, teens are more likely than adults to play electronic games, but electronic gaming is still very popular among adults as well. While most grandparents may be reluctant to play with their enthusiastic grandkids, some do. If not, it is a good bet that they at least *watch* in amazement.

Guy Buckmaster regularly plays the game *Guild Wars* with his children as a way to stay connected to them. Adults with kids are more likely to play video games. *(Source: AP Photo/Steve Nesius)*

(Everyone 10 and older) have content that may be suitable for ages 10 and older. Titles in this category may contain more cartoon, fantasy, or mild violence, mild language and/or minimal suggestive themes." "[And] titles rated T (Teen) have content that may be suitable for ages 13 and older. Titles in this category may contain violence, suggestive themes, crude humor, minimal blood, simulated gambling, and/or infrequent use of strong language."[6]

Recent research on teens and video games has shown that 97 percent of teens between the ages of 12 and 17 play some type of video game.[7] Which devices and games are the most popular? Specifically, 86 percent of teens play on a console such as the Wii, Xbox, or PlayStation, while 73 percent play games on a desktop or a laptop computer. Also more than half (60 percent) use a portable handheld device such as the Sony PSP or Nintendo DS, while just under half (48 percent) use a cell phone or other PDA to play games. Clearly, consoles remain the preferred way to play games. As for types of games, research has also shown that teens play a number of different genres, especially gamers who play daily. For example, almost half (40 percent) of teens play eight or more types of game genres.[8] The most popular games among teens was the rhythm game *Guitar Hero*, the first-person shooter game *Halo 3*, the sports game *Madden NFL* (football), the casual card game *Solitaire,* and the rhythm game *Dance Dance Revolution*. While this was only one study, it reveals popular games played by teens include several genres and with varied ESRB ratings. Therefore, contrary to public opinion, the most popular video games are not all blood and guts and full of violence and profanity.

ADDICTIVE ASPECTS OF ONLINE GAMING

At what point does one truly become addicted, and what are the addictive aspects of gaming? When answering these questions, it is important to think about the reasons why people play games in the first place. People play online and electronic games for mental stimulation, competition, escapism, socialization, and connection with others, and simply because it is fun. In general, people are good at things they like to do. Conversely they like to do things they are good at. In electronic gaming, most games allow people to experience new things even though they are in fantasy worlds or environments. As they experience higher levels of success they are challenged in greater ways. Very few games are designed to allow players to actually "win." Rather, they are designed to induce more fun and more game play. In the process a player's sense of fun can run even deeper to satisfy greater psychological needs or levels of personal "growth" (e.g., confidence, independence, or self esteem).[9] Players may also realize a sense of power and control as when they defeat an enemy, beat a sports team, drive a race car or monster truck, or navigate a virtual world by collecting valuables.

While all of this bodes well for game manufacturers and players alike, the great allure and corresponding amounts of time needed to experience ever-increasing levels of satisfaction can lead to addiction. After all, a main goal of game designers is to design games that people want to play and play often. This seems especially true when considering specific genres such as MMOGs, which are often designed to motivate players to keep coming back for more. The premise is basic: The more interesting, challenging, exciting, and enjoyable the game, the more time (and money!) players will spend, especially when there is no end to the game. No one can rightfully claim they actually won *World of Warcraft*, because this is impossible—the game just keeps going on and on in ways that induce continued playing and paying.

Besides the many recreational reasons for playing, what else about online gaming makes it addictive? According to the Web site http://www.video-game-addiction.org, games are often designed at just such a level as to be challenging, but also designed so that the player is rewarded with small achievements to keep them playing. The famous psychologist B.F. Skinner called a very similar process "shaping," which is a system of using little rewards to train someone (in this case a gamer) to continue on with a given process. Little rewards represent achievements, such as completing a game level or collecting a virtual item of value. Very similar to playing casino games like slot machines, little wins get players to believe the next one will be even bigger and better. This makes it easy to push a video slot machine button labeled "maximum bet" while thinking the next turn will return a really big payoff. It can be very difficult for some players to "turn themselves off" and tune out just when they "know" they are about to win really big.

Other addictive aspects or hooks of online and electronic gaming include trying to get the high score, or trying to get to the next level, or, as previously indicated, trying to "beat" the game. Games like the popular *Super Mario Brothers* include trying to make it through many different levels, called worlds, by running and jumping over (or on) numerous enemies while keeping focused on the end goal of saving a princess. For some players this can involve hours upon hours of repetitive game play to achieve the master level, or to succeed at individual levels and to move through worlds in the game space. Repeated game play meets the ultimate objective of game designers, which is to keep the players engaged in patterns of activity that are continuous and seemingly never-ending. It is for the same reason that newer versions of games are periodically released. And there is nothing inherently wrong with any of this, provided individual players are sufficiently educated, remain aware, and, in the case of children, are properly supervised so they can enjoy appropriate kinds of games in healthy ways.

ADDICTIVE TYPES OF GAMES

So what types of games are the most addictive? The ever popular MMOGs are often cited as the most addictive in nature. This may be a cause of concern as the gaming industry seems to be increasingly moving toward MMOGs that require subscriptions and that call for continuous pay and play. The Voice of Internet Gaming (VOIG) Web site (http://www.voig.com) estimated the total number of subscriptions for these games at approximately 50 million in 2008, and the number is probably increasing.[10] Exploding popularity pertains to potentially addictive properties of many, though not all, MMOG games. In general, time spent playing a game improves one's chances of being *more* successful, while not putting in the time makes it difficult to keep up with other players. Gaming researcher Nicholas Yee noted other reasons that people are drawn to play MMOGs. Many of these games, for example, allow for escapism, a sense of achievement, socialization, and the ability to manipulate players within a game space. Other researchers agree with Yee but think that problem use of MMOGs has more to do with immersive aspects of escapism rather than a person seeking pleasure in the game. In addition, perhaps an even more important hook is the social aspect of the game.[11] Many and lasting friendships are created in gaming environments. Games also provide opportunities to find new friends who share passions and who have similar or complementary skills needed to succeed in team play. Accordingly "little successes and rewards" to advance in the game often contribute to addictive behavior. The implication is that, left to their own unregulated passions, players can become hooked through socialization processes endemic to game play rather than only as the result of fantastic digitally programmed content designed to enhance players' excitement. This probable reality adds to concerns about never-ending MMOGs that have no ultimate goal, final mission, or way to "win."

Other factors that researchers have found useful for predicting MMOG addiction include curiosity, need for reward, a sense of belonging, obligation or sense of duty for community, and role-playing that involves being attached to a particular game character. Drastic examples of young people assuming or trying to emulate characteristics of their favorite avatar *in real-life* demonstrate just how powerful the influence of some games can be. Overall, research now suggests that aspects of gaming content, along with gamer behaviors (such as amount of time spent), their sense of satisfaction while playing games, and their interrelationships with fellow gamers may lead toward addiction.

Joyce Protopapas of Frisco, Texas, can attest to the addictive aspects of online gaming. Her 17-year-old son, Michael, played video games on a daily basis for two years. She noticed that video games and the Internet transformed him from an outgoing, academically gifted teen to a reclusive manipulator who flunked two 10th-grade classes and spent several hours a day playing the online video game *World of Warcraft*. Joyce noticed in her son some of the same addictive behaviors that her alcoholic husband displayed. She brought her son to therapists and tried to take the game away, but

Joyce Protopapas noticed negative changes in her son's behavior as he became immersed in the game *World of Warcraft*. Although MMORPGs are often cited as the cause of online gaming addiction, other types of video games have the potential to develop into an addiction. *(Source: AP Photo/ Donna McWilliam)*

Michael would just threaten his family and act in a possessive manner. Michael eventually spent six months in a therapeutic boarding school, but it is unknown if this cured his addictive tendencies. This case represents just a small segment of the number of cases that include youth and adults who become consumed to the point that they fall behind in their work, school, or personal life. According to a report prepared by the American Medical Association's Council on Science and Public Health, overuse most often occurs with online role-playing games involving multiple players. *World of Warcraft* is considered the most popular, teen-rated, multiplayer, role-playing game.[12]

While MMOGs often get the most attention when considering addictive potential, other online multiplayer games and single-player role-playing games carry that potential as well. For example, these games also require a substantial amount of time and practice to obtain sufficient levels of skill so as to be recognized by other online gamers. The competitive nature of these games, especially those that include tournaments or ladders, often includes keeping track of win-loss records. Therefore players will keep playing to get a competitive advantage or to otherwise get ahead of the other players. Similarly, such games may be addictive because if players lose progress or their standing in the game, they may need to spend even more time and/or play with greater intensity in order to make up their losses or regain their standing before the game is "saved" and stored.

Additionally, non-MMOGs may also have addictive social aspects as friendships are developed with other players via online and/or off-line interactions. All games not played alone and in isolation may require players to collaborate to achieve success. This too requires investment of time, a lot of time in some cases. Consequently peer pressure may become a factor as players entice, dare, or threaten one another to stay involved. Extreme cases may involve aspects of cyber-bullying as players intensify their need or that of their team to achieve greater success. Hence, players often feel compelled not merely to play, but to play often, hard, and harder still. Negative reinforcement like this contributes to addictive tendencies of players. Thus, compulsive, problem, and addictive gaming involves characteristics of gamers themselves and the choices they make with regard to what to play, how often, with whom, and under various circumstances.

TRAITS OF ADDICTED GAMERS

Online games have qualities that may contribute to or cause addiction, but what is it about the gamers themselves? Can people possess certain biological, psychological, emotional, or behavioral traits that cause them to be at greater risk to becoming addicted to online and/or electronic games? The short answer is "perhaps," though scientists are a long way from providing specific or convincing evidence of this. Yet a small but growing number of researchers are investigating potential risks and harms associated with electronic gaming, and many people believe they themselves are addicted to one or more forms of electronic gaming or believe they know someone who is. For example, Kimberly Young, a recognized expert in Internet addiction and founder of the Center for Internet Addiction Recovery, described certain psychological characteristics that may predispose some gamers to addiction. These include low self-esteem, fear of rejection, or needing a high degree of approval by others. Young suspects that a number of other personal characteristics are related to gaming addiction such as intelligence, imagination, social shyness, and the tendency to engage in abstract thinking. Other potential individual characteristics positively related to risk of addiction may include loneliness, being overly self-conscious, and having issues with social anxiety.[13]

Researchers have also found that depression, isolation, and anger are often associated with online gaming addiction, while a lack of a sense of belonging and social acceptance among peers may also factor into the onset or continuation of addiction in individuals. Similar to other "addictions," such as to sex, gambling, or eating, people may use gaming as a way to help them cope with some type of inner emotional pain. Researchers have also noted that a person's gender, age, personality type, skill at playing one or more particular games, family structure, and playing habits may also influence their risks for becoming addicted to MMOGs.[14] The purpose here is not to list, much less explore, all personal risk factors, but rather to point out that there are many reasons why people may become "addicted." It is also important to understand that people at risk may become more at risk when combinations of factors become present in their lives. Consider a person who ordinarily enjoys playing a game 10 hours per week, but when stressed in school may feel a need to escape by spending more time gaming online. Even so, this individual may only feel this "need" for a short period of time before getting back on track with priorities in their life. Moreover, most gamers never experience what could reasonably be considered compulsive gaming, problem

GAMERS SUPPORT AS WELL AS COMPETE WITH EACH OTHER

In a recent suicide case of a gamer, Mitchell S., also known as "Kuja105," fellow gamers got together to locate information about the gamer who was depressed and considering ending his life to convince the individual not to do it. Kuja105 posted a message in the gaming forums including those on http://www.GameFAQs .com and http://www.MetalGearSolid.org that he wanted to end his life, citing that he was overwhelmed with school and his finances. Fellow gamers responded to his post urging him not to take his life and tried to convince him that things would get better. Members of the forum sought out contact information and spent countless hours on the phone with him pleading to him that suicide was not the best option. Sadly, Mitchell ended his life by consuming anti-freeze and painkillers.[15] Even though Mitchell ended his life, it can be seen that many members of gaming forums come together and treat fellow members like their second family.

gaming, or an addiction to gaming. Further, although members of gaming forums can be manipulative and offensive to fellow players, individual gamers and groups of gamers are also known to provide support when fellow gamers signal a need for help.

Popular culture offers many references to online gaming communities and stereotypes of online gamers. Often depictions of gamers on television or other media stress crudeness and rudeness rather than sensitivity, genuine friendship, and support, which also exist in abundance among gamers. The television show *South Park* featured an episode entitled "Make Love, Not Warcraft," which parodies many aspects of online game addiction. The producers of *South Park* also created an episode called "Guitar Queer-O," which features a made-up game called "Heroin Hero," in which people developed a drug-like addiction after playing the game. *The Simpsons* also mocked gamers in an episode titled "Marge Gamer" in which Marge suffers from overuse of an MMORPG. Web comics also provide references to the gaming community and addictive nature of online gaming. The Web comic *Ctrl+Alt+Del* has a story about a character's addiction to the game *EverQuest*.

While pop culture may unfairly ridicule gamers and point to prospects of gaming addiction, the sad reality is that people throughout the world are presenting themselves to friends, family members, counselors, and treatment professionals for help for what they or people close to them believe may be a problem with gaming. This state of affairs compels thinking and caring people, especially those in positions of authority or trust, such as parents and teachers, to become more aware of and sensitive to the allure of online and electronic games, as well as the many positive and some risky things that gamers themselves do.

RELATIONSHIP BETWEEN PLAYING MMOGS AND PIU

A recent study investigated connections between playing MMOGs and problematic Internet use (PIU). Researchers Scott Caplan, Dmitri Williams, and Nick Yee noted that commonly accepted symptoms of PIU include using the Internet for maladaptive mood regulation, compulsive use, preference for the unique social interactions that occur online over those that occur off-line, preoccupation with the Internet, and real-life problems due to Internet use. It has been well established and documented that PIU is related to being lonely, depressed, anxious, shy, aggressive, introverted, and deficient in social skills. In their study, however, these researchers found that the strongest predictors of PIU were age, Internet use patterns, and psychosocial well-being.[16] Interestingly, they also discovered in this study that both achievement motivation and social motivation were *not* significant predictors of PIU, though MMOG gaming is. Specifically the strongest MMOG-related predictor for PIU was immersion in game play. Thus escapism appears to be a very important reason that people chose to play MMOGs. But too much of anything can be unhealthy.

The next strongest predictor for gaming addiction was the use of voice technology, probably because of its ability to instill a sense of community from online relationships. When players actually talk among themselves during a game, human connections become stronger. This in turn builds players' commitment to each other and their sense of community. Finally, this study reinforced the findings of previous research that the desire for psychosocial well-being and a sense of community may contribute to PIU. People who are lonely, introverted, or depressed often turn to the Internet to cope.

THE ATTRACTION OF GAMING

Kids and adults enjoy playing video games for a variety of reasons. Whether as friends, classmates, coworkers, or family members, people love playing games with each other online and by themselves electronically. In a study about the issue of motivation and emotion, investigators from the University of Rochester and Immersyve Inc. (a consortium of researchers and development professionals who have researched online motivation and engagement) reviewed what motivated 1,000 gamers to continue playing video games. Richard Ryan, a motivational psychologist from the University of Rochester and lead investigator of the study, stated that there is more to gaming than the theory that people play for the fun of playing. During the study, gamers were divided into four groups and asked to play different games. Researchers found that games can provide opportunities for achievement, freedom, and even a connection among players. As a result, gaming provides more than just a simple sensation of fun. Gamers also enjoy challenges and feel great about themselves when they connect their gaming to their real-world knowledge, skills, and relationships.[17]

Several factors, however, typically constitute addictive aspects of gaming. Combinations of biological, psychological, social, and environmental aspects may influence a person's addictive tendencies. Something as simple as an increased chemical response in a person's brain, an adrenaline rush, relief of stress, or feelings of belonging as a result of playing a game can lead to becoming "hooked." Researcher Nick Yee believes that causes of addiction may be either negative *motivational factors*, such as real-life problems, stress, or low self-esteem, or positive *attraction factors*, such as achievement or relationships. But addiction is also about meaningful experiences such as discovery, rewards, sense of belonging, or duty (e.g., to a community or in the sense of patriotism). Role-playing as when a gamer assumes the identity of a character can also be thrilling but harmful if excessively pursued. Therefore online and electronic gaming can be addictive because it involves physical, psychological, and/or emotional aspects. *Cultural* factors such as conforming to social networks and expectations of how technology should be used can also be important when considering addiction and its causes. Digital youth culture is especially important when considering addiction because of its emphasis on "friending" while competing and learning via online relationships that include interactive game play. The opposite can also be true: Not playing online and electronic games in modern society means going against societal trends, which may lead to a person becoming socially isolated online and/or offline.

CONCLUSION

Regardless of correlations to and causes of addictive gaming, and whether or not gaming is truly addictive for people who seemingly play in excess, addiction in all its forms is about behaviors that become harmful as the result of a person losing control. Addicts are people who, through excessive consumption or engagement of something, experience harmful consequences in one or more areas of their life. Physical, psychological, and/or emotional harms from excessive online gaming can be very real and destructive. Whether the addictive source is a drug, food, gambling, sex, or electronic gaming, the condition or possibility of an addiction must be taken seriously. And while it may be easy for people who are not "addicted" to ask someone who is, "Why don't you just stop?," addictions are never easy to kick. If kicking a habit was easy, compulsive players would not risk or sacrifice their finances, health, and school or job responsibilities much less personal relationships for "just a game." The same holds true for addiction to online gambling.

Internet Addiction and Gambling

Life is about taking necessary risks. Gambling, however, involves betting money unnecessarily for fun and/or to get money quickly without actually earning it. Alex began betting on sports when he was only 13 years old. Initially he casually bet his friends via conversations and texting, but in time he used the Internet to inform himself about the odds of certain teams or athletes winning particular sporting events. Like nearly everyone who gambles for any length of time, Alex lost money and was also tempted to spend more time gambling and to place larger bets to make up for losses. Of course, this strategy did not work. In short order Alex's debts grew, his schoolwork suffered, and so did his relationships with friends to whom he owed money. Recognizing Alex was often late for school and not doing well in his classes, school officials tried to contact his parents. But Alex intercepted letters sent home and would erase phone messages left on his parents' answering machine. Things got worse when Alex began to steal from his friends, his family, and even from the family business to pay for his gambling losses. It was only when the family discovered they were missing money that they realized Alex owed money and that he had a gambling problem.[1]

The story about Alex is not unique, nor is gambling limited to sports betting online or off-line. According to a major study completed by the National Research Council (NRC) in 1997, "[g]ambling in America has deep cultural roots and exists today as a widely available and socially accepted recreational activity." At the time of this study, "over 80 percent of American adults reported having gambled sometime during their lifetime—on casino games, lotteries, sports betting, horse racing and offtrack betting, and other gambling activities." In that year the NRC estimated that Americans alone wagered more than $551 billion, creating a vast and intensely competitive interstate gambling market.[2] Today gambling in some form is legal in nearly all U.S. states, and the gambling industry is among America's largest and most profitable. It is also true that millions of adults responsibly engage in recreational gambling as a form of entertainment, and that trips to places such as Las Vegas, Nevada, which actively promote gambling, are enjoyed by entire families even though children themselves cannot legally partake.

Despite widespread enjoyment and economic booms in many states derived from legal gambling, many people object to gambling for religious or personal reasons, given likely financial and other types of harm brought about in most cases of extensive gambling over long periods of time. Such reasoning makes very good sense because odds of winning always favor establishments that provide gambling services. Sooner or later the "house" always wins! Besides, who has ever heard of a gambling casino going broke?

Consistent with such logic, the NRC pointed out in its 1997 study that gambling does indeed have many social and economic costs. Of particular concern are the number of adults and young people who become problem gamblers and even pathological gamblers. These people have great difficulty resisting temptations to gamble even though gambling causes harm to themselves, family members,

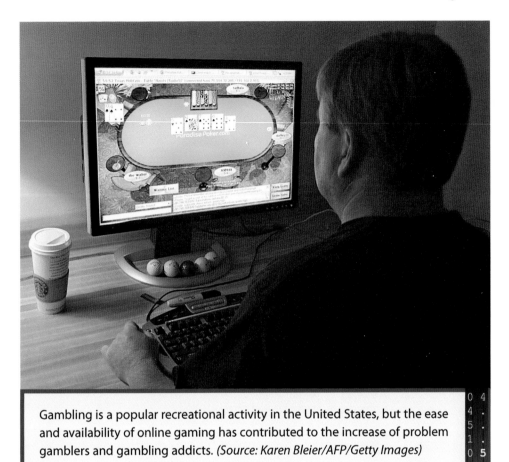

Gambling is a popular recreational activity in the United States, but the ease and availability of online gaming has contributed to the increase of problem gamblers and gambling addicts. *(Source: Karen Bleier/AFP/Getty Images)*

coworkers, and friends. This important study also concluded that the Internet and computerization is changing the technological nature of gambling in disconcerting ways, with more people gambling and wagering more. Today nearly 2 million American adults and more than 1 million American adolescents between the ages of 12 and 18 likely suffer from pathological gambling, a disorder of impulse control recognized by the American Psychiatric Association.[3] Notably connections between pathological gambling and so-called Internet addiction remain unclear to researchers and mental health treatment professionals. Nonetheless, substantial and increasing numbers of people throughout the world are seeking help for online

PATHOLOGICAL GAMBLING

Pathological gambling as determined by the American Psychological Association (APA) is a medical condition suffered by people who have five or more of the following symptoms:

- committing crimes to get money to gamble
- feeling restless or irritable when trying to cut back or quit gambling
- gambling to escape problems or feelings of sadness or anxiety
- gambling larger amounts of money to try to make back previous losses
- having had many unsuccessful attempts to cut back or quit gambling
- losing a job, relationship, or educational or career opportunity due to gambling
- lying about the amount of time or money spent on gambling
- needing to borrow money to get by due to gambling losses
- needing to gamble larger amounts of money in order to feel excitement
- spending a lot of time thinking about gambling, such as past experiences or ways to get more money with which to gamble

gambling problems, which in lay terms and understanding may be considered an important form of Internet addiction.

SOCIAL AND ECONOMIC COSTS OF GAMBLING

Michael was 43 years old, with a wife and two young children. He was on the fast track to a great career in corporate finance and enjoyed using the computer both at work and home. For Michael, life seemed perfect, and he was happy with both his profession and personal life. However, Michael was spending countless hours playing online poker at home and at work. Typically after a long day at work, Michael would come home, quickly enjoy dinner with his wife and kids, and then rush upstairs where he would play poker until 3 or 4 A.M. Consequently, he progressively suffered from lack of sleep, which caused him to perform less well in his job. He also missed many evenings of homework time with his kids and communicating with his wife. Hence Michael's compulsion to play poker was eroding other and more important aspects of his life. Although Michael began to play online poker with fake money on various Web sites, in time he switched to betting real money from his family's savings account. When his wife Susan found out, she confronted Michael and reminded him their savings were intended for their children's education. Sadly, Michael continued to gamble in hopes of winning back his losses. In the end Michael sought counseling for his Internet gambling addiction. With counseling and family support he came to accept that he had lost control of his life. Having hit rock bottom, he decided to spend more time with his family and in time began to use computers again responsibly both at work and to help his kids with homework.

Michael was one of thousands of adults who, at any given time, are addicted to online gambling. The thrill and excitement associated with the Internet and gambling often entice people to gamble online more and more. It is necessary, however, to distinguish boundaries and rules so that important aspects of life, including family and friends, are not neglected as a result of excessive Internet or online gambling activities.

GAMBLING BEFORE AND AFTER COMPUTING AND THE INTERNET

Before computing technologies entered mainstream society, gambling and gaming mostly consisted of face-to-face interactions. People gambled with cards and poker chips or placed live bets on sporting events or horse races. People also met in casinos, local town halls, pubs, and race tracks to place bets and partake in poker or other card games. The thrill of winning could be seen whenever a person shouted with glee. Security then, as now, was handled by people who walked around and monitored both the players and the people managing the games. As the Internet became increasingly popular in the 1990s, so did the realization that the Internet could be used for gambling. Opportunities for Internet gambling began to grow in 1996, when Intercasino, based in Antigua, became the first online casino to accept real bets.[4] Quickly thereafter additional online casinos, lotteries, and sports betting Web sites came about to offer a tremendous variety of Internet gambling opportunities.

Nowadays most reputable online casinos and gaming sites are licensed and somewhat regulated by the countries where they are hosted. As such they are limited in their use of technology to set odds of winning and to enhance betting experiences in ways that keep people coming back for more. This means that in-facility and online gambling machines are carefully programmed to allow gamblers to sometimes win some money, but rarely in large amounts.

Within traditional casinos, surveillance technology enables security workers to monitor players' every move. But technology used in traditional and online casinos helps owners monitor players' winnings and guard against internal theft by employees. The slot machines, mechanical card shufflers, and table games in traditional casinos are infused with or surrounded by computing technology to generate a sense of gambling "action," i.e., indoor atmospheres pumped up with colorful lights and catchy sounds that smack of fun and winnings to be had. Everything about the inside of casinos—from the maze-like carpet designs and floor planning of gambling machine and table locations, to an absence of windows and clocks, combined with tableside service of food and (intoxicating) beverages—is designed to keep gamblers focused on betting.

INCREASING POPULARITY OF ONLINE GAMBLING

Today personal computers and portable IT devices like smart phones also provide users with 24–7 Internet gambling. People using such devises can visit online casinos whenever they wish from the comfort of their own homes or other familiar places. Once online they can engage in many forms of betting that closely resemble slot machines and card games traditionally offered only in real casinos or other kinds of betting establishments. Online Casino City (http://www.onlinecasinocity.com) now describes and ranks more than 2,000 online casinos and betting sites, including virtual poker rooms, bingo parlors, lotteries, and sports betting opportunities. Popular games played online include blackjack, video poker, video slots, roulette, and craps. Although online betting establishments can only mimic real-life gambling facilities, they now attract millions of gamblers worldwide who possess a great variety of skill and tolerance for taking risks while playing games of chance.

IS ONLINE GAMBLING RISKIER THAN OFF-LINE GAMBLING?

It is reasonable to believe that, given the convenience and variety of online gambling, it will continue to grow in popularity. The ability to gamble online anonymously, just like in real casinos and other kinds of betting establishments, also holds promise for growing the popularity of online gambling, though many countries, including the United States, require gamblers to report their winnings as income for tax reporting purposes.

Conceivably online gambling will cut into profits to be made through traditional off-line betting and gambling-related tourism markets. But there is something fundamentally different about online gambling, which can be done from anywhere, versus traditional gambling that takes place within physical establishments like casinos, off-tracking betting locations, and bingo halls. Comfortable places like the privacy of one's home may reduce inhibitions that naturally work to protect gamblers from over-betting. Consider so-called pajama gamblers (as when a person at home gambles in their pajamas). Perhaps such gamblers can more easily become addicted precisely because they do gamble alone in isolation. After all, such individuals have few if any social constraints or oversight to impinge on potentially reckless gambling behaviors. In addition, online betting is easy. It requires only that a person: (1) visit a gambling Web site, (2) establish an account using a valid credit card (as "proof" of age and to set a credit limit), and (3) click away. Future visits require users to merely login to continue gambling. Also, online gambling players need *never* get dressed, go anywhere, interact with dealers or other gamblers, handle money or betting chips, pull a slot machine lever, or risk being taken in by "action environments" for which casinos are so famous. Instead online gamblers can rest comfortably in the isolation of their own thoughts, surrounded by anything imaginable, with hopes of winning and perhaps winning big. Certainly they *may* be able to interact with other players depending on technological capabilities (e.g., Web cams). Yet there is something odd and limiting about gambling under such circumstances, especially when comparing this to traditional forms of gambling that are historically prevalent in societies and cultures throughout the world. As such, online gambling in isolation may pose greater risks of slipping into conditions of problem or pathological gambling lifestyles. Regardless, it is unlikely that the Internet and the online forms of gambling it enables reduces risks of gambling, especially since they allow so many more people to gamble in the first place.

CONNECTIONS BETWEEN PROBLEM YOUTH GAMBLING AND GAMING

Regardless of whether gambling occurs online or off-line, too much gambling can be very detrimental on a number of levels. Further, given similarities between gambling and gaming (e.g., competitive risk taking), distinctions between problem-pathological gambling and problem gaming and perhaps even pathological gaming, though not officially recognized as a medical disorder, may be rooted in an obsession with stakes and methods of betting rather than other factors such as competition in risk taking. Perhaps this is the very reason why pathological gambling, which can occur through traditional

YOUTH GAMBLING

Research about online gambling indicates that online gamblers tend to be younger than people who gamble in traditional venues. Online gambling rates are higher on college campuses than in society as a whole, but the types of games played relates to player age. For example, people older than 30 prefer online betting on sports and horse racing. In a study of European sports betters, it was found that online poker players tend to be 26 to 35 years of age, while the average age of online casino players was 46 to 55.[5] Other studies have found the overall average age of online gamblers to be in their mid-30s.

According to research by the University at Buffalo's Research Institute on Addictions (RIA), gambling activity is widespread among youth and young adults between the ages of 14 and 21. The study involved surveying 2,274 youth from all across the United States over a two year period. Results showed that 11 percent of youth surveyed stated that they gambled at least twice per week, while 68 percent of youth reported that they had gambled at least once in the last year.[6]

The rate of problem gambling among young people between the ages of 14 and 21 was found to be 2.1 percent, which equates to about 750,000 young people. In addition, young people were found to be more likely to gamble if they held a full-time job, were *not* in school, and lived on their own. Interestingly, problem gambling was almost nonexistent among female adolescents. While this study did not specifically look at online gambling, other research has indicated ranges of 6 percent to 9 percent of students who have reported gambling online.[7]

and online forms of betting, is a diagnosable disorder but online and electronic gaming addiction is not officially deemed to be a medical disorder.

Even so, people who suffer from pathological gambling in adolescence and continue gambling into adulthood nearly always bet more and with higher stakes as their financial resources increase. It is widely understood that for most users computing begins early in life with gaming activities. Also, many MMORPGs and other types of games played online involve betting money in conjunction with social computing activities integral to digital youth culture. Therefore young users must be wary of their potential to slip into uncontrolled gambling that begins as mere gaming in either off-line or online ways. Parents and other adults who are responsible for supervising children's online gaming should also be on the lookout for competitions that involve secret betting. In other words, some gamers bet off-line on their online game play.

ONLINE GAMBLING AND PATHOLOGICAL GAMBLING

The influx of computing technologies at home, school, and the workplace allow gamblers to gamble in inappropriate ways or places. Internet technology also makes many forms of gambling possible regardless of a user's location, including offtrack betting on races and card games like poker or blackjack or other types of casino action. Computing has allowed gamblers to bet at any time of day. Cell phones come equipped with games such as blackjack or poker and can even allow a person to connect to other gamblers to place live bets on card games while they are at a work or meetings or another activity. Numerous Web sites exist that simulate casino-style gambling activities such as blackjack, poker, and slot-style online machines. Gamblers just need an Internet connection and credit cards to gamble away their fortune at any time of day.

Like those who might be addicted to alcohol or other drugs, pathological gambling is a chronic disorder that is very dangerous without treatment. Even with treatment, many patients still resort to gambling. One of the best ways to prevent such behavior is to avoid areas in which gambling occurs. This can be quite a challenge for those using computing technologies because cell phones, personal computers, and gaming consoles are everywhere, offering opportunities for gambling.

PROBLEM GAMBLING AND AN NBA REFEREE

Tim Donaghy seemed to have it all: a family he cared about and a great high-profile job as a National Basketball Association (NBA) referee with a high salary that most people would love to have. However, his supposed wonderful life blew up on him after he was caught breaking the law and NBA rules by betting on NBA games. How could he possibly throw his life away over sports bets? For him, it began with simple bets on golf games and escalated to the point where he

was making high-stakes bets in casinos and on sports games, including the very games that he officiated and could influence. After spending 15 months in prison, Donaghy stated that he accepted responsibility for his actions and tried to send a positive message to other problem gamblers that help is available. He said that he did what he did because, in the back of his mind, he always had the need for more excitement, thrills, and action, and as a result had an impulse to engage in risky behavior. The risks were double for Donaghy, as he not only risked losing money on bets but also risked his reputation and career. Ultimately, he lost both.

NBA referee Tim Donaghy became involved in a gambling scandal when officials discovered that he was providing insider information to his bookies. Donaghy, a gambling addict, had been unable to cover his debts and was trying to earn his money back. *(Source: AP Photo/Louis Lanzano)*

Perhaps the closest phenomenon to pathological gambling, or gambling addiction, is compulsive video-game playing. Both have similarities beginning with the idea that they are behaviors that involve playing games. As such, people may play both for similar reasons, such as entertainment, to experience emotions, or because it is intrinsically satisfying. They may play games or gamble to relax, or to experience an adrenaline rush, or to escape from the daily concerns and stresses of life. Both can contain random elements, and both use a system of reinforcing rewards to keep people playing. These rewards are designed to tap into the compulsive nature of people. After all, how many people play slot machines and spend all of their money despite knowing they are getting small wins that will keep them playing and eventually take all of their money? Those small wins create the sense that it is their lucky day, and that that luck will result in winning great fortunes. The urge to go for the jackpot is too great, despite the odds being stacked against them to win. Little by little, the small wins start to diminish until the player has next to nothing. Then the player has to "go for it" because what's the point in leaving with just a few dollars? Gambling and game playing are not pathological activities by nature, but they can become so if they cause personal or social problems.

Douglas Gentile from Iowa State University used the DSM-IV criteria for pathological gambling to conduct a study about pathological video-game use among youth between the ages of 8 and 18. For the study, he modified the criteria for video games. From a national sample of youth, results showed that 8.5% of young video-game players exhibited "pathological patterns of play" as indicated by answering "yes," "no," or "sometimes" to questions about their gaming habits.[8] They were considered a pathological gamer if they exhibited 6 out of the 11 symptoms. Some of the symptoms, in order of prevalence, were:

- skipping household chores (33 percent said yes to this question, 21 percent said "sometimes")
- playing to escape problems or bad feelings

- skipping homework assignments
- doing poorly on schoolwork or tests because of playing
- lying to family and friends about how much they play
- needing to spend more and more time and money to feel the same amount of excitement
- trying to quit without success
- becoming restless or irritable when trying to cut down
- stealing games

CONCLUSION

The Internet has greatly expanded the number of opportunities for people to gamble online. The very nature of Internet gambling, however, creates the potential for more people to become addicted. For example, the simple convenience of being able to access computers and gamble from anywhere at any time in relative anonymity can be a problem for some. Another issue that can be problematic is the idea of playing with electronic money, which can create a sense that it is not "real" money. In addition, Internet gamblers who gamble at home may find it easier to gamble under the influence of drugs or alcohol because there is no worry about being in public. Gambling while intoxicated decreases the ability to make circumspect decisions about betting and wagering money. Finally, there is increasing research-based evidence that people who gamble using the Internet are more likely to be problem gamblers.[9]

Other Digital Addictions
and Obsessions

Katie is a 24-year-old woman just beginning her career in graphic design. She graduated with high honors from a well-known university and is quite excited to begin to work for a popular magazine. After receiving her first big paycheck, she realizes that she can buy a few new outfits for work and a few other new items that she has been waiting to buy until she found a job. During her lunch break she hops online to pick out a few outfits and sees all of the great online deals. A few days later she receives her order in the mail with no problems and is quite thrilled by the ease of shopping online. Not only does she feel great in her new outfit at work, but she also feels great that she is finally earning a respectable paycheck.

Within the next few days Katie decides to look online for more clothes and shoes that she can wear to work. She enjoys receiving special offers at her work e-mail address about sales and the latest styles. Katie decides to buy more clothes while she is on the clock and signs up for more special offers to be sent to her work e-mail. Within her first two months on the job, Katie has spent the majority of her time at work shopping online and signing up her work e-mail for various offers. She has also spent most of her earnings on new clothes. After Katie missed a few important meetings because she was too busy typing in her mailing address for an online order, her boss requested to meet with her to discuss her work performance.

While meeting with her boss, Katie admits to her latest excitement in online shopping and the thrill it gives her to receive packages at home after work. Her boss explains to her how much of her habit is affecting the company's revenues and tells Katie that if she does not immediately stop shopping online during work hours, she will be fired. Many people enjoy surfing the Web or playing games while they are at work and in most cases, believe that they can easily do both without impacting their work productivity. Sadly, in some cases, employees are being terminated for online browsing during work time.

Technology has developed so rapidly over the past 20 years that it has significantly changed how people live their lives. Capabilities of a modern cell phone, which most people now have, far surpass those of the hulking giant computers of the 1960s that existed only in select government, military, or educational settings. Software applications seem limitless, and once installed on computers or cell phones, enable people to communicate and engage with each other from anywhere in the world. Through the Internet people socialize, research, shop, learn, work, share, teach, play, and seek entertainment. All of this can be very exciting. This change is not always positive, however. The countless number of activities that can now be so easily done online has created issues with more people becoming addicted to certain kinds of Web content or to specific activities carried out on the Internet. As the technology has become smaller, more portable, and mobile, it is reasonable to believe that more people will have difficulties with overuse, obsession, or addiction.

EXCESSIVE USE OF MOBILE DEVICES

Car phones and first-generation cell phones were originally developed to use in emergencies. People could dial 911 for help rather than having to walk miles to try to locate a gas station with a coin-operated pay phone. If a person was stuck on a highway or if they were in unfamiliar territory, it was up to them to try to find help or hope that a helpful traveler would stop and provide assistance. Today, however, most people carry a cell phone. As a result, traveling to distant and unfamiliar territory has become less scary because people can rely on their cell phone as a lifeline in an emergency.

As of 2008, the number of people throughout the world carrying a cell phone was in the billions. Roughly 60 percent of the world utilized a cell phone in their everyday life. Younger individuals are now using cell phones. Whereas it was common in the beginning of the 2000s for college age students, parents, and professionals to purchase and utilize cell phones, it is now common for young people in elementary school to own and use a cell phone or even a smart phone with applications and a data plan that allow users to listen to music, watch TV, and even play electronic games while on the go.

Smart phones today often come installed with applications that provide global positioning system (GPS) locating on maps, texting, and travel guide services to help users locate the nearest gas station with current prices or nearby restaurants and types of food they serve. As a result, cell phones have become much more than just tools for emergency situations. With data plans that now include Web browsing, texting, e-mail (into which pictures, video and Web links can be inserted), along with streaming music and movies, smart phones are actually mobile "mini-computers" that allow people to stay in touch while being entertained wherever they are. Some people are now using cell phones as they would a laptop computer and because of that they are constantly relying on its data services to search for information and stay connected. And technology companies that make smart phones are continually working to expand their functionality, communication range, memory, and operating speed so that customers feel more and more inclined to use their devices as much as possible.

Youth and adults enjoy using the many features of today's smart phones. But with constantly improving features and product availability, teens and adults may also be tempted to use smart phones when not appropriate, such as when driving a car or while in a classroom. Using a cell phone in a manner that is not hands-free as when text messaging is dangerous to everyone on the road. Many states and some countries now prohibit texting while driving. Further, talking or even texting with a phone during a meeting or other gathering of people may be disruptive and rude. Users of any kind of IT device need to be mindful of the circumstances and their surroundings before answering a call or booting up a device.

Yet staying connected is important and simple for all ages thanks to the vast array of cell and smart phones available, and mobile devices allow people to communicate whether they are free to speak or not. Generally the subjects of most messages include mundane things such as how one's day is going, planning events, and gossip. Even so, some users feel compelled to send or respond to messages at all times of day or night regardless of their circumstances.

Whereas it was once common to whisper a secret, texting now allows people to send "secret" messages usually without others knowing it is happening. As a senior, Harry attended high school in the day and worked part time some evenings and on weekends in an office supply store. Harry was consumed with using his smart phone while at school, work, or just hanging out alone or with friends. With his device tucked away in a shirt pocket and ear buds affixed, he felt he could go anywhere and do anything while being entertained and staying connected. One day after school Harry attended an office meeting at the store where he worked. He and several other store employees convened around a table while the office manager talked about new products the store would be selling, anticipated changes to store hours and employee shifts, and the importance of providing sound and friendly advice to customers. Harry could not care less. He had worked at the store for nearly two years, and he had heard this kind of speech several times before. So instead of remaining professional, Harry cupped his phone in the palm of his hand and tapped out a message to a coworker friend sitting on the other side of the table in the same room. Unfortunately for them, the manager saw what was going on and subsequently reprimanded both employees. Harry and his friend were also shunned by other employees who were offended by their texting during the office meeting.

Many youth choose to text rather than speak to their peers even while sitting right next to each other. This is not really very different than adult coworkers in adjacent offices exchanging e-mails rather than speaking to one another face-to-face or by

GROWING USE OF CELL PHONES

The research is clear: The majority of teens prefer cell phones as their primary means of communicating with each other. Texting rather than speech, however, is the new norm for how teens reach out to each other. According to the Pew Research Center's Internet and American Life Project, 75 percent of 12- to 17-year-olds owned cell phones in 2010, as opposed to only 45 percent just six years earlier. More than half of the teens surveyed text daily, with one out of three teens sending more than 100 messages a day, which equals more than 3,000 texts per month.[1]

Young people and adults are also more likely in the future to access the Internet and perform other activities more often by using a cell phone rather than another type of IT device. In 2010, 54 percent of *all cell phone* users used their phone to send photos or videos, 23 percent accessed a social networking site with their phone, 20 percent used their phone to watch a video, and 15 percent posted a photo or video online through their cell phone. Cell phone activity usage increases markedly when considering only adults ages 18–29 years old. Among users in this age group, telephone. Where should users and society "draw the line" between what is socially acceptable use of IT devices and what is not? Can extensive use of cell and smart phones for professional as well as for personal, social reasons lead to excessive use that becomes harmful to users themselves or other people with whom they must interact face-to-face?

Greg Hardesty is a reporter for the *Orange County Register*. He found out the hard way that cell phones and texting can be very addicting for young people. His 13-year-old daughter texted 14,528 messages in a single month. This phone activity resulted in a 440-page AT&T cell phone bill. Greg was furious and also concerned. He asked his daughter who she was texting to, and she said, "A

95 percent send or receive texts, 93 percent use their phone to take pictures, 81 percent send photos or videos to others, 65 percent access the Internet on their phones, 60 percent use their phones to play games or record a video, and 48 percent use their phones to access a social networking site.[2] Clearly, people are using portable phones more, and for more kinds of communication and recreational activities. Much of the usage is social in nature. Hence the concept of social computing and social networking via the Internet is becoming increasingly popular, the new norm for users of all ages. A future challenge for individual users, and perhaps especially for younger users who enjoy social computing so vital to digital youth culture, will be to gauge the extent to which they rely on and feel compelled to use IT devices and the Internet. This is in relation to actual or potential harms caused by or correlated with extensive use of technology. Users must also consider and compare the relative benefits of face-to-face interconnections with people for personal as well as professional reasons. Striking a balance between IT-enabled versus face-to-face interactions seems sensible, but is probably not seriously considered or acted upon by many people who are at risk of experiencing harmful consequences from using IT devices and the Internet excessively.

lot of my friends also have unlimited texting so I just text them all the time." Greg's daughter averaged 484 messages a day, which is one text message every two minutes during every hour she was supposed to be awake rather than sleeping. If Greg did not have an unlimited text plan his phone bill for the month would have been $2,905.60 in texting fees alone. But as a concerned parent, Greg realized that his daughter simply could not have been paying adequate attention in school, and simply must have been nearly constantly texting her friends even while with them. Parents like Greg and adult guardians are right to be concerned about excessive use of smart phones and other IT devices by their children. Frequently they wrestle with balancing how much and under what circumstances children should be allowed to use devices and the Internet. Luckily for parents, cell phone companies offer "unlimited texting" plans.

Another safety issue related to the prevalence of cell phone use among young people and adults is texting while driving. In November 2009, New York State placed a ban on texting while driving. If caught, drivers in the state of New York face fines of up to $150. This ban followed a state ban on talking on one's cell phone while driving. Currently nine states, Arkansas, California, Connecticut, Delaware, Maryland, New Jersey, New York, Oregon, and Washington, along with the District of Columbia and the Virgin Islands have handheld cell phone bans for all drivers. With the exception of Washington State, a police officer may ticket a driver for using a handheld cell phone while driving without any other traffic offense taking place. As of July 2011 no state completely bans all types of cell phone use for all drivers (e.g. police officers on duty may be exempt). However, 34 states, the District of Columbia, and Guam ban text messaging for all drivers. In some states, such as Maine, New Hampshire, and Utah, speaking on a cell phone is only an offense if the driver is also committing some other moving violation, excluding speeding (called secondary enforcement). For example, if the person was pulled over for swerving in and out of traffic, the person can also be ticketed for using a cell

Texting is quick and easy, and many people believe that they can text while performing other activities, such as driving or working. More than a dozen states, including Washington, D.C., have enacted bans on texting while driving. *(Source: AP Photo/Jim Cole)*

phone. On the other hand, 31 states have primary enforcement for text messaging, meaning that an officer may cite a driver for texting without any other traffic offense taking place.[3] Still, the safety issue associated with distraction from texting is not limited to motor vehicles. In 2008, a deadly collision occurred between a commuter train and a freight train that was blamed on an engineer who missed a stop signal because he was texting.

COMPULSIVE SHOPPING

The Internet has made the task of picking out a new outfit or purchasing a new DVD much easier. Stores that might not be located close by or are only open for limited hours make it challenging to buy merchandise. The Internet, however, has broken down those geographic boundaries and made shopping possible at any time of day or night. Online stores can also have an increased selection that might include extended sizes, limited editions, and rare designs. The Internet has also made shopping much easier for those who are considered "compulsive shoppers."

A compulsive shopper is one who enjoys shopping but may not think about the effects of their purchase, such as if it falls within their budget. Compulsive shoppers who use the Internet have a greater ability to make irrational shopping decisions at home or at work. They might feel the need to purchase the latest CD or designer shirt that is on sale for only a short time online. Stores send "special one of a kind" discounts directly to their customers' e-mail to further entice shoppers to spend money at their Web site. Such offers can cause people to purchase items they do not need. This can be quite dangerous because unlike physical malls and stores, online stores do not close and are ready and willing to take a customer's hard-earned money at any time.

One of the biggest shopping days of the year has now adapted and become more "online" friendly. Black Friday, the day after Thanksgiving, is considered the biggest shopping day of the year, and many stores offer impressive bargains that day. Black Friday now includes many online specials in addition to early morning in-store specials. Instead of waiting outside of stores in the early morning hours, customers can go online to their favorite stores' Web sites and receive online bargains. For the "new" Black Friday, many families delegate certain family members to go out to the stores in the early morning hours and others to shop online at home in the early morning hours to receive online specials.

Cyber Monday, a term coined by the National Retail Federation in 2005, is the first Monday after Black Friday. Cyber Monday is the official online shopping day for the holidays and offers shoppers substantial savings similar to those of Black Friday. Even though more people have begun to shop online, in-store shopping continues to lead in retail sales. For example, in 2007, Cyber

Monday had a total of $881 million in sales as opposed to Black Friday, which took in $41 billion in revenue.[4] Many well-known stores have improved their Web sites and prepared themselves for Black Friday shopping. In 2009, the quality of online stores tracked on Black Friday improved from 2008, and there were fewer outages and issues affecting customers, according to Ben Rushlo, director of Competitive Research at Keynote, a company responsible for Internet performance management services. In 2009, the best-performing sites included Walmart, Sears, and Barnes & Noble.[5]

Online shopping has also allowed young teens to purchase items that might not be appropriate or allowed by their parents. Anyone can type in "porn" or "condoms" and find sites with such items for sale. In many cases it is quite easy for the experienced, underage shopper to find a way to purchase such items. Purchasing alcohol online while still underage is a common occurrence among young teens. By easily going to the Web sites of various liquor or beer stores, they can have alcohol shipped directly to their dorm room or apartment without being asked for age verification.

Students at the Gonzaga University in the state of Washington conducted an experiment in 2004 on whether online stores would sell to minors and if so, what the reaction of local law and government officials would be. The underage students ordered liquor, beer, and wine and had it delivered to their homes without being questioned about how old they were. After being able to purchase the alcohol, they went to then-State Attorney General Christine Gregoire to explain how companies such as Costco.com are selling alcohol to minors.[6] The issue raises a serious debate about alcohol control and interstate commerce. As e-commerce is on the rise, the sale of liquor online is becoming more popular. However, if such regulations are not properly handled as they are with in-store purchases, then law enforcement is not enforcing an equal standard of the law. A liquor store owner could be fined and have their store shut down if found selling alcohol to minors, and yet online retailers may receive no punishment for selling to minors online. Of

Retailers often use the Internet to promote special sales and promotions. The popularity of Black Friday, the biggest shopping day of the year, inspired the creation of Cyber Monday, an online sale event. *(AP Photo/Paul Sakuma)*

course, the more important issue is that Internet sales of alcohol are allowing minors to obtain a substance they are not legally allowed to purchase or consume.

OTHER ONLINE OBSESSIVE BEHAVIORS

Computing technology could lead to other forms of obsessive behavior. Take for instance watching a favorite television show. Improved telecommunications and wireless technology allow viewers to easily record and watch a program at their convenience by texting to their DVR which show to record. Even better, they can pause and resume the show with a few simple clicks. This can make watching a favorite television show a simple and easy activity. Computing technology acts as just another "tool" similar to other forms of technology that allow a person to easily engage in a behavior. If multiple shows are recorded, however, and an individual becomes consumed with attempting to watch them at the expense of other areas of their life, then this is problematic.

Computing technology also makes it easier to engage in devious behavior. Take for instance the concept of stalking. Before social networking sites, texting, GPS, and other forms of computing technology, a person had to rely on face-to-face interactions and "pound the pavement" to track down another person. Now one can simply stalk a person by viewing their multiple status updates or GPS location broadcast through their cell phone, or even check their streaming Web cam image. Stalking, in and of itself, is often obsessive because a person will stop at nothing in order to have a relationship with someone who does not want to have a relationship with them. The technology facilitates the obsessive behavior because it creates so many different ways to either contact them directly, or "watch" them online from afar.

SEXTING, PROMISCUOUS SEXUAL CONTENT, AND PORNOGRAPHY

Sexting is the act of sending sexually explicit pictures, images, or messages via cell phone. The constant connection of young people via mobile devices combined with their risk-taking behavior and sexual exploration is concerning. Research by the Pew Research Center's Internet and American Life Project has found that 15 percent of teens who own phones have received sexually suggestive nude images *of someone they know* via text message. People may engage in sexting for a number of reasons, including sexual exploration or because it is exciting or fun. Yet some "sexters" send messages to people they do not even know, perhaps because they want to get to know them or be in a relationship with them. This can have obvious legal implications as those who receive unsolicited pictures can be considered victims, especially when they are minors.

Sometimes people engage in sexting that involves the exchange of images between people (often a couple) that are then shared outside of the relationship. It is these types of situations where sexting can also become cyberbullying. When messages that are supposed to be private are shared with others, the results can be emotionally devastating. This is often the case after a relationship has ended, as most young relationships do, and emotions run high. The problem is that even after the relationship is over, the sexted images remain and can be used as a weapon for revenge. In one tragic case Jesse Logan, an 18-year-old high school senior from Ohio, sent nude photos of herself to her boyfriend. After they broke up he forwarded the pictures to other girls, which resulted in her being bullied and physically assaulted. She committed suicide as a result.

Before computing technology and cell phones, promiscuous sexual content could also be easily found in magazines, television ads, movies, and commercials. Companies used sexual content to lure customers into purchasing products. It is easy to notice on television how sexual content is salted into music videos, commercials, and television shows. In addition to television shows, sporting events also use promiscuous sexual content to attract a larger audience. Sports teams spend thousands of dollars on cheerleading squads that wear minimal clothing and perform to songs in a sexually suggestive manner. Even when unintended, sexual content creeps into programs intended for all ages. For example, Nielsen estimates that 6.6 million kids age 2 to11 were watching the 2004 Super Bowl halftime show when Justin Timberlake ripped off a piece of Janet Jackson's clothing, exposing her right breast to the nationwide audience. Another 7.3 million teens age 12 to 17 were tuned in at that time as well. In addition, in a sample of programming from the 2001–2002 TV seasons, sexual content appeared in 64 percent of all TV programs. Those programs had an average of 4.4 sexually related scenes per hour. Talk of sex in TV programs is more frequent (61 percent) versus overt portrayals (32 percent). One out of every seven programs includes a portrayal of sexual intercourse.[7]

The Internet has provided a new outlet for media to expose youth to sexually explicit content. Youth can utilize the Internet to privately satisfy their curiosity about sex without having to ask their parents. The Internet not only provides text about sexual behavior but also graphic images and videos. Youth can engage in communication about sexual behavior with their peers away from their parents while doing research online. In some cases this can be beneficial as teens can feel more comfortable discussing sexual behavior with their peers via text or instant message.

Pornography can be found all over the Internet. Pop-ups, spam e-mails, Web sites, and chat forums may include pornographic images and text with Internet users. Even with numerous filters, blocks, and other forms of antispam software, a person still can be subject to sexually explicit content. Pornography does not discriminate as to the people who view the content and thus young people can easily be subjected to explicit material with a few clicks of the mouse. When a teen views such content, it can affect their opinion of what is normal, healthy sexual behavior and what is not.

No matter what the location, the use of promiscuous sexual content to enhance tangible items is common. Cell phone companies offer the latest model as a tool to get a new number or to stay in contact with a current crush. In car ads, car companies depict the latest model as the tool to attract women. Even companies that sell toothbrushes or office supplies try to entice customers through promiscuous sexual appeal. As a result, it is evident that the Internet would only bolster and recycle this content for users across the globe to see.

The legality of pornography on the Internet—with the exception of child pornography—is still unsettled. According to the federal government, one can determine if a video or picture is considered pornographic with the Miller test. The Miller test dictates that community standards are to be used in determining whether particular content is obscene. If a community determines that the work is pornographic, it could be banned. Something that might be deemed obscene in one state may not necessarily be considered obscene in another state. This poses a significant challenge when such pictures are uploaded onto the Internet because they become available everywhere.

The federal government's first attempt in regulation of pornography occurred with the creation of the Communications Decency Act of 1996, which prohibited the "knowing" transmission of "indecent" messages to minors and the publication of materials that depict, in a manner, "patently offensive," as measured by community standards. Sexual or excretory activities or organs are often but not always protected from access by minors. Immediately after this act was put in place, the American Civil Liberties Union argued that the "indecent transmission" and "patently offensive display" provisions limited freedom of speech guaranteed by the First Amendment. The U.S. Supreme Court in the case *Reno v. American Civil Liberties Union* struck down the law. A second attempt was made with the narrower Child Online Protection Act, or COPA, of 1998. This law forced all commercial distributors of "material harmful to minors" to protect their sites from access by minors. "Material harmful to minors" was defined as materials that by "contemporary community standards" are judged to appeal to the "prurient interest" and that show sexual acts or nudity. Several states have since passed similar laws.

Another act intended to protect children from access to Internet pornography was the Children's Internet Protection Act, also known as CIPA, of 2000. This act required that public libraries, as a condition of receiving federal subsidies for Internet connectivity, employ filtering software to prevent patrons from using Internet terminals to view images of obscenity and child pornography and to prevent children from viewing such content. While the intent of these laws is well meaning, it has not limited the number of pornographic sites that now exist online. The Internet now contains an abundance of pornography, much of which can be viewed or downloaded for free. It can fuel a strong desire of an Internet pornography viewer who can eventually become addicted to this behavior.

CONCLUSION

The Internet provides myriad opportunities to do many things. Most cell phones now come with the ability to connect to and access the

ADDICTED TO PORNOGRAPHY

According to Dr. Dave Greenfield of the Center for Internet Studies, one should not underestimate the addictive potential of the Internet and the psychological effect it can have on people.[8] Greenfield also believes that, similar to addictive substances, one can develop a tolerance for the excitement and stimulation of Internet activities. This means that it can take more and more time spent online to achieve a level of stimulation that was achieved through less time previously. This can also be the case when considering the viewing of pornography online. In one case a 29-year-old professional male named "Fred" found out that the Internet can be very addictive. In most phases of his life Fred was successful and he also had a long-time girlfriend to whom he was hoping to get engaged. However, Fred was also addicted to online pornography.

According to Dr. Greenfield, when he first met Fred, he was spending numerous hours both during and after work viewing pornography. He even planned his business trips around having Internet access or access to an adult video store. He spent hundreds of dollars on online pornography, bought sexual products online, and was even a victim of theft as someone was able to use his credit card due to his online activities. He described himself as being out of control and obsessed and unable to stop. This feeling of losing control left him feeling afraid, and this led him to seek help. The lure of the Internet was just too much to handle on his own, but he was able to find help through therapy.

Internet, as well as other activities such as taking and sending pictures, watching videos, texting, and of course making phone calls. The tremendous growth in the numbers of those who use the Internet and own cell phones has coincided with incredible technological change. This is a cause for concern when thinking about people who can become addicted to all that the technology has to offer. It is not the technology that they are addicted to but what the technology enables them to do. In other words, the activities are addicting. Certain people can become addicted to just about anything, such as work, gaming, gambling, sex, shopping, exercise, television, music, and yes, computers and the Internet. With the Internet, it can be more problematic because it creates instant and convenient access to any number of pleasurable behaviors. Most people are able to balance their lives and engage in a number of activities in a healthy way. There are others, however, who fall victim to an addictive pattern that results in real harm and consequences.

Potential Consequences and Other Dangers

In 2007, 23-year-old Tanya Maree Quattrocchi from Melbourne, Australia, was convicted of posing as the American Idol 2004 runner-up Diana DeGarmo to send e-mails to DeGarmo's friends and family. In addition, she texted DeGarmo 570 times and called her 369 times in three months. She further stalked the singer by contacting her relatives and others, and according to the Victoria police, viewed DeGarmo's MySpace page 700 times in a six-month period. The judge, Lisa Hannan, ruled that victims such as DeGarmo "had no doors to lock and no alarms to activate," and sentenced Tanya to one year in prison.[1]

In another case, in March 2005, 41-year-old Qiu Chengwei stabbed to death fellow online gamer Zhu Caoyuan in Shanghai, China, for selling a virtual cybersword for 7,200 yuan that the men had previously jointly won in an online auction. Reportedly Chengwei loaned the dragon saber to Caoyuan, but reported it to police as being stolen after learning that Chengwei had resold it for the equivalent of $870. At the time of the murder Chinese

*intellectual property laws had no provisions for determining right-
ful ownership of the virtual sword or its value, because although
players must invest time and money to acquire such virtual property, such assets constitute data for which there exists no legally
admissible proof of ownership or legally recognized estimates of
market value.[2] Nonetheless Chengwei was convicted of murder. He
received a suspended death sentence, which meant under Chinese
law that he could spend between 15 years to the remainder of his
life in prison.[3]*

Depending on where they live and societal norms, people suffering from addiction may be regarded as either victims and/or the
cause of their problems. For many people the timeless debate about
who or what is to blame for addictions is important but likely will
never be resolved throughout society as a whole. However, millions
of people suffer social and economic consequences stemming from
obsessive behaviors of their own or of people such as family members, coworkers, or friends who spend too much time online. In
direct and indirect ways individuals, organizations and even communities at large must bear the costs of health care, criminal justice
services, and social dysfunction brought on by addictions.

CONSEQUENCES OF INTERNET ADDICTION AND EXCESSIVE ONLINE GAMING

Whenever a person becomes addicted to a substance, activity, or
content there are consequences that affect them personally. These
are known as *direct harms.* When family members, coworkers, fellow students, or friends are affected by a person's addiction, *indirect
harms* result. A third category of consequences are called *tertiary
harms.* These are harms that affect people throughout entire communities and society at large, even if they did not interact with or
know the addict or victims of indirect harm. Direct, indirect, and
tertiary harms all involve social and economic consequences. These
are easily understood but often difficult to measure in monetary
costs. Even so they are important for understanding the consequences of addiction it all its forms.

Singer Diana DeGarmo was cyberstalked by an Australian woman who managed to hack into DeGarmo's MySpace account and e-mail. The cyber-stalker also obsessively called and texted the singer. *(Source: AP Photo/Peter Kramer/file)*

Direct Harms of Internet Addiction

Direct harms of addiction are those that are experienced by the addict. Examples of direct harms that may also include symptoms of addiction are:

- preoccupation with an addictive substance or activity, which with gaming would include constantly thinking or talking about a game even when not playing it
- inattention to household, school, or work-related responsibilities in favor of engaging in the addiction
- rationalizing or lying about the amount of time spent playing games
- sleeplessness or irritability, especially when unable to engage
- losing interest and involvement with other things or people that were once enjoyed
- forgoing eating, sleeping, or relieving oneself in order to continue playing
- stealing money or other items to sell in order to spend more money (and time) playing a game

Any or all of these direct kinds of harm or symptoms of addiction may occur to lesser or greater degrees, in short or longer periods of time, and may be more or less recognizable by the addict themselves or by other people with whom they associate. Addicts who go without eating, sleeping, or bathing are easier to spot than those who mask or deny their problem by staying physically healthy and keeping up their appearance.

Another thing about direct harms is that some involve greater consequences than others, and these too may come about progressively in different ways over time. A gaming addict may initially spend inordinate amounts of time playing, eventually lose interest in other hobbies or sports, and eventually lose non-gaming friends and not promote past a grade in school because of their habitual gaming.

Other addictive behaviors that may occur with addiction to online gaming, or another form of Internet-enabled addiction, include overeating, smoking cigarettes, drinking excessive amounts of alcohol, or abusing prescription or illegal drugs. It bears repeating that all of these addictions by themselves or in combination may cause direct harms to the individual doing such activity. Consequences of addiction often include damaging mental or physical health, compromising or destroying relationships, suffering in school, losing employment, depleting financial resources, and experiencing legal difficulties, among many other kinds of consequences. Fortunately, when a person discontinues his addictive behavior, he is probably able to restore himself in many ways and ideally before the consequences of his actions are ruinous. In other words, addictions of all kinds are to be avoided and the sooner they are quit or diminished the more likely and able a person is to recover. Conversely, the longer an addiction is allowed to go on, more harm and lasting damage is likely to occur.

Self Destructing Online

How many people have stayed up for numerous hours playing a new video game they bought? They not only might have lost track of time but might also have missed out on other activities in which they would normally engage if they hadn't purchased or overused the game. Missing sleep or forgetting to do homework as a result of overplaying a video game is not in itself evidence of addiction. However, doing this to an extent that school performance or other responsibilities or relationships suffer indicates a problem, perhaps an obsession, and even addiction that requires professional assistance. Whether one is addicted to activities or content enabled by a personal computer, cell phone, or other device, direct harms can result, and when this happens intervention is required.

Video game packages include health and safety warnings similar to those found on alcohol or cigarette packages. In some countries a booklet that contains important information about one's health and safety while playing a video game is included. Most gamers ignore and toss these booklets aside as they quickly open the box to play the game. Similar to those who smoke or consume alcohol, gamers seldom if ever worry about potential harms to themselves or others.

LATE-NIGHT GAMING

Research has shown that excessive gaming can cause sleep disorders. For example, online and electronic gamers, using both computers and consoles, who feel that they are "addicted" sleep few hours and experience feeling tired more often than non-gamers and casual gamers.[4] Thus the more hours spent playing games, the less sleep players were getting. According to one 28-year-old gamer:

> I have been told many times that I play too much. Usually, I don't see myself as playing too much, but there have definitely been times I have felt I should be doing something better with my time. I'm sure there have been plenty of nights where I could have, and should have, gotten much more sleep instead of playing video games. In the long run, though, it didn't affect me much such as hurting job productivity or anything. On the other hand, spending way too much time playing definitely had a role in the breakup with an ex-girlfriend. That is one of the moments where I did feel that I played too much, and where I also realized that my priorities were not in the correct order they should be.

As shown in this story, lack of sleep is often just one issue related to playing too much. Another consequence of excessive gaming can include damaged romantic relationships, often due to the fact that someone would rather play games than be with their significant other.

Nintendo shares all of its precautions and warnings listed about their games on their Web site for consumers to read. Warnings include that some gamers may experience seizures, repetitive motion and eye strain, electronic shock, and motion sickness. Nintendo cautions gamers to, "Take a 10- to 15-minute break every hour, even if you don't think you need it."[5] For most committed gamers, a break after only an hour of play would be excessive and unheard of as they enjoy playing nonstop for countless hours. Furthermore, many people assume such warnings are placed only as legal precautions instituted by lawyers of gaming companies, and frankly do not care about them.

It has been reported that people have died as a result of excessive gaming. However, it was not the game that killed them, but rather lack of sleep or not eating that occurred due to their excessive gaming behavior. According to the Associated Press, a 30-year-old man living in Southern China died from "an overdose" of online gaming. The man had played games nonstop for three days at a local Internet café and fainted. He was pronounced dead by paramedics soon after. Other similar cases have occurred in all parts of the world. The BBC reported that a South Korean man died from exhaustion after playing games for 50 hours straight, and the Web site Gamespot.com reported, in 2002, that a gamer was found dead in an Internet café's restroom after playing games for 86 hours straight.[6]

Gambling and Overspending

The thrill of hitting the "jackpot" can entice one to try their luck playing a card game or slot machine at a casino. Flashy machines, complimentary drinks, and a lack of clocks can make someone feel like they have only been inside a casino for a short time. Casinos remain in business by making money. This occurs only by disappointing gamblers' hope for riches. Traditional casinos feature many kinds of table games and slot machines through which to entice gamblers. Well-dressed dealers along with food-and-beverage servers encourage gamblers while making it easy for them not to leave the game. Complimentary drinks and a hope to win "big" drive many gamblers to overspend despite losing vast sums of money.

Online gaming casinos attempt to mimic traditional casinos by creating exciting, if only virtual gambling environments. Indeed computing technologies and the Internet now enable gamblers to test their luck while playing from home or even when traveling.

COMMITTING A CRIME IN ORDER TO GAME OR GAMBLE

For some gamers, their desire to play or bet can result in excessive spending and lead to stealing in order to maintain their gaming obsession. In 2007, police in Vietnam arrested a 13-year-old boy accused of murdering and robbing an 81-year-old woman. The boy told the officers that he needed money to play online games and he decided to kill and rob to do so. After killing the woman he stole 100,000 Vietnamese dong or roughly $6.20.[7] Just like others addicted to a certain behavior, some problem and pathological gamers condone illegal acts to gain money so that they can continue their habit.

Web sites offer a variety of gambling experiences that simulate being in a fancy casino. This enables gamblers to engage anytime they can access the Internet. As with traditional gambling casinos located in places like Las Vegas, Nevada, or Atlantic City, New Jersey, unwary Internet gamblers risk experiencing direct consequences of addiction if their recreational gaming becomes problematic or pathological.

INDIRECT HARMS OF INTERNET ADDICTION

It is easy to predict and spot direct harms experienced by addicts. Like throwing a ball into the air, everyone knows that it will quickly fall due to gravity. Addicts also quickly or eventually fall down in their lives in many ways, as evidenced by the direct harms they experience. It is harder to see indirect harms that are caused by an addict, however, because by definition these are experienced by other people such as family, friends, and coworkers of an addicted person. Even so, indirect harms experienced by one or more people may have as many, or even worse, overall consequences as direct harms experienced by a single addict.

Consequences of Addiction Experienced by Family and Friends

Family, friends, classmates, and coworkers also suffer from addiction in other people, because they have to live with addicts and the disruptions they cause. It is no fun being around addicted people who are consumed with their own interests at the expense of others. Of course the Internet provides a wealth of information and has something to pique anyone's interest. However, when totally committed to an online game, social networking site, shopping experience, or other activity, a person reduces their otherwise available free time and/or money to spend with friends and family. An addict's overriding need to check MySpace or get to the next "level" of a new game can leave a friend or family member feeling unimportant. In some cases it can make them think twice about planning activities with an addict even if the addict is a loved one. And when male Internet users become addicted to pornography, wives and girlfriends may naturally feel less intimate and attractive, and wonder how they can possibly compete for attention from the person they love.

Overuse of computing technologies can make one so distracted that they do not see how much time they are wasting and not spending with family and friends. This can cause disagreements over many things beyond online behavior and lead to missing out on social events. In such cases people who are addicted will generally make up excuses to allow them to continue their behavior and keep falling behind on their family and friends because they feel that their family will always be there to support them and the game or online activity is more important at that moment.

Compulsive gaming in particular can also impair life functions in other ways. Anecdotal evidence exists in stories about gamers who stopped eating or showering or even made temporary "toilets" near the computer so that they don't have to leave the game. As previously mentioned, a warning sign for compulsive gaming is preoccupation with a game (i.e., thinking about and talking about it even when not playing). For a non-gamer, the person who constantly talks about warlocks, ogres, quests, and raids may seem eccentric. Most non-gamers do not even know what a guild is. Other warning signs include lying about how much time they play, losing interest in real-life activities, and losing interest in real-life relationships.

Consequences of Addiction Experienced by Classmates or Coworkers

Similar breakdowns in relationships can occur between an addict and their classmates or coworkers. Having to accomplish projects with people who are not able to perform their responsibilities can be aggravating, to say the least. Regardless of the type of relationship affected, added indirect harms often include feelings of disappointment, sadness, anger, distrust, or betrayal. These feelings can complicate even legitimate misunderstandings that take place at home, school, or work, and lead to disagreements over any number of things or even physical violence. In short, addictions of others frequently have consequences that indirectly harm people affiliated with those afflicted with addiction.

Online gaming, compulsive shopping, and excessive use of social networking sites can all lead to lack of productivity in school or a workplace. When one is consumed with online activities, the need to continue such behaviors can be disastrous. Imagine a surgeon who enjoys using Twitter and checking Facebook. Would a patient feel comfortable if the surgeon took a break to "tweet" about how their day was going? While this is an extreme example, many employees in various jobs actively use their computing devices to maintain Internet addictions. Robert Half International, which specializes in professional employment staffing, conducted a survey that revealed 55 percent of executives believed that time spent surfing the Internet for nonbusiness purposes is undermining their employees' effectiveness on the job.[8] Businesses can purchase software and hire IT security employees to track Web traffic, but those who might be abusing their Web privileges can find ways around such restrictions, especially by using personal IT devices that are not monitored via company-owned information systems. Many companies now require employees to sign a code of conduct form that clearly instructs what employees may or may not search for or access while on the job.

TERTIARY HARMS OF INTERNET ADDICTIONS

Tertiary harms are those experienced by society at large, but may also include effects and costs of coping responses engaged in by addicts. Coping responses are the ways in which people compensate for the direct and indirect effects of their addictive behavior. For example, someone who is addicted to the game *World of Warcraft*

People who are constantly exposed to digital devices and gadgets may have trouble living without them. Psychologists say that a rise in technological addiction among the youth in Asia is resulting in negative consequences. *(Source: Roslan Rahman/AFP/Getty Images)*

and as a result sees their grades and social life suffer may blame such actions on others, rather than themselves. They might blame the difficulty of the class rather than their lack of effort because they are spending the majority of their time playing the video game. Such coping responses can prevent one from truly understanding the addictive nature of their own behavior and from beginning to treat such behavior as a problem. Through their coping responses, they convince themselves they have no problem. In addition, if an addicted student fails a class and standardized tests required by government, the reputation of a teacher may also suffer. By extension entire schools and communities suffer if government funds to support education are reduced. This example may seem an exaggeration when considering the effects that a single addict may have, but when the consequences of addiction in all its forms are added up, the magnitude of tertiary harms becomes more apparent and disconcerting.

ONLINE DANGERS RELATED TO INTERNET ADDICTION

The Internet has many useful aspects that allow people to communicate, learn, and engage in global business. With any medium such as the Internet, however, there are dangerous aspects as well. Cyberabuse consists of, but is not limited to bullying, cheating, pirating, identity theft, computer hacking, password cracking, sexting, and various other forms of online deviance or crime. It is important to be wary of the many forms and ways in which cyberabuse and cybercrime occur in order to help protect hardware, data, oneself, and other users who share information systems. When it comes to online safety and security, irresponsible practices including many forms of Internet addiction may indirectly expose other users to online threats.

Research conducted by Dr. Samuel C. McQuade and other professionals at the Rochester Institute of Technology that focused on the ways in which thousands of kindergarten through 12th-grade students use IT devices and the Internet revealed a startling reality: Users most prone to addiction were those who engaged the most in online gaming, and these individuals were also most likely to engage in various forms of online abuse and cybercrime. This striking finding is consistent with an abundance of research that heretofore has focused on addiction-related online gaming and gambling largely to the exclusion of crime. Linking Internet addiction with excessive online gaming and gambling along with cybercrime underscores a need to consider possible connections between addiction and various potential dangers of being online.

Cyberbullying and Cyberstalking

Cyberbullying occurs when a person uses IT to embarrass, harass, intimidate, threaten, or otherwise cause harm to individuals targeted for such abuse. Cyberbullying amounts to a technological extension of physical bullying that has traditionally been carried out face-to-face or indirectly over the telephone or through typed or handwritten messages. Regardless of the technologies employed, bullying has traditionally involved one person or multiple aggressive people who seek out victims they perceive to be weak or vulnerable, and then pick on them over time. Increasingly bullies are using IT devices to carry out their activities. Cell phones, laptops, and electronic gaming devices have all facilitated bullies in transmitting their messages to their victims. At the same time victims of bullying constantly wonder what is being communicated about them in text messages, e-mail, Web postings, and so on. Victims of cyberbullying constantly worry about what will be posted next. They live in a state of fear, regardless of whether actual physical harm has already or could occur. Indeed traditional physical bullying like face-to-face name calling, shoving, and playing mean-spirited pranks often occurs right along with cyberbullying.

The concept of cyberstalking, like cyberbullying, is not new and employs many of the same methods and technologies as cyberbullying. Like cyberbullying, stalking online has become easier to accomplish with IT devices and the Internet. The key difference is that while cyberbullying may take place once or even several times over short or long periods of time, and involve individual bullies, groups of onlookers, and groups piling-on to abuse the victim, stalking, whether in person or online, nearly always involves a single perpetrator and occurs with increasing intensity over time. This means that, whereas cyberbullying may and often does intensify if not stopped, cyberstalking will always intensify until it is stopped. This is because stalkers are usually motivated by sinister things such as revenge, sexual fantasies, celebrity fascination, and/or violence. Hence the stalking may be defined as, "the willful, malicious and repeated following and harassing of another person."[9] But the concern in the context of Internet addiction is that cyberbullying and cyberstalking and an obsession with the thrill of victimizing others may become integral aspects of a person's life online—a predominant focus of their computing activities. What for some begins as an impulse eventually becomes a practiced and irresistible art to bully or stalk, however sinister the intentions or consequences. The worst offenders likely lose perspective of themselves in their disregard for victims.

As computing devices become less expensive to purchase and easier to use, more potential bullies and stalkers are able to carry out their activities just as more individuals are susceptible to becoming victims of both cyberbullying and cyberstalking. Individuals are creating online profiles and spending hours online playing games, chatting with friends, and joining social networking groups. Young people spend countless hours on sites such as Facebook updating their profiles, commenting on their friends' pages, and adding visual content such as pictures, audio, or videos. This behavior not only further exposes teens to potential offenders, but may also create or at least contribute to addictive tendencies associated with feeling the need to keep up with their peers about what is happening online. As a result, sharing personal information on social computing forums provides cyberbullies and cyberstalkers with plenty of information about their victims and thus creates further dangers for Internet users of all ages.

Other Forms of Addiction-Related Cyberabuse

The Internet has provided a new avenue for criminals to steal personal information. Before the Internet, one had to be concerned about a person pickpocketing, dumpster diving, or burglarizing a home or office to obtain personal documents or information. The Internet allows a person to steal sensitive information from a distance, remotely, virtually, and therefore in most cases without a person's knowledge. Once sufficient personal information is acquired from any number of online sources (as well as hard-copy documents), identity theft and other types of online credit card and bank fraud can occur rather easily. Identity theft, for example, happens when a person takes personal information such as someone's Social Security number, name, or credit card account number, without consent, to commit fraud or other crimes. According to the Federal Trade Commission (FTC), an estimated 9 million Americans have their identities stolen each year.[10]

Phishing occurs when cybercriminals manipulate people into giving away personal information that can then be used to commit various types of online fraud including identity theft. In most cases the victim is tricked by an e-mail or text message that urges her to visit a fraudulent Web site. Once on the Web site, users may falsely become convinced of the importance of sharing personal, financial account, or computer password information. The process is normally monitored by hostile computer systems located in foreign countries from which cybercriminals can operate with little fear of being investigated much less arrested by police.

The Gartner group, a technology research company, estimates that the direct phishing-related loss to U.S. banks and credit card issuers in 2003 was $1.2 billion.[11] Indirect losses, which include losses that customers of financial institutions face as a result of such attacks, can be even more damaging. In most cases replacement costs to repair and protect customers' identities and their overall trust in the financial institution can range in the millions, depending on the size of the institution. This is really important because sometimes cyberstalkers, and even cyberbullies, as in cases involving spousal divorce, may employ phishing to commit financial fraud against their victims as another form of threat, intimidation, or harassment.

Other potential dangers exist for those that use the Internet excessively and either intentionally or unwarily divulge confidential information. Obviously knowing a user's password allows an offender to hack or trespass into her online account(s). Password guessing and cracking results in the same thing. By obtaining the password, a bully or stalker can access a variety of additional confidential or personal data and use it for their own gain, as well as to cyberbully or cyberstalk perhaps through implanting malware (malicious software) such as viruses, Trojans, or worms on their victim's computer. Malware is often designed to infiltrate and damage a computer system without the owner's knowledge, or to enable remote spying of a user's online activities.

Keystroke logging or "keylogging" is a special kind of software that has legitimate uses (as when used by system administrators to monitor for inappropriate computer activity) and illegitimate uses as when cyberoffenders, including cyberbullies and cyberstalkers, use it to monitor in real time what their victims are doing online. With such knowledge, they can plan their next moves—when and

KEYLOGGING CONTROVERSIES

While keylogging is a potential danger for Internet users, it has also been used as a tool for law enforcement. In May 1999, the Federal Bureau of Investigation obtained a warrant to secretly break into the office of Nicodemo Scarfo Jr. Nicodemo was involved in racketeering, illegal gambling, and loan sharking with his family. FBI agents installed a keystroke logging tool onto Nicodemo's computer after being unable to view an encrypted file during a clandestine search of his office one month earlier. The keystroke logger allowed FBI agents to discover the file's password and access the encrypted file. The warrant required that the software did not monitor Internet traffic, because monitoring one's Internet browsing would be equivalent to obtaining a wiretap.[12] This controversial case provided both prosecutors and defense attorneys' a new look into what the government believes is acceptable in obtaining private information of the general public. James Dempsey, deputy director for the Center where to go, and what to do when they arrive, in order to further threaten, intimidate, or harass their victims. Obviously the more time a person spends using their IT device (especially keyboards), coupled with not adequately protecting their device and system from malware, including keystroke logging applications, the more vulnerable they are to becoming cybercrime victims.

CONCLUSION

The Internet offers users many ways through which they can mentally "wander off" and become distracted. Done in moderation, exploring the Net can be interesting, enjoyable, useful, and rewarding. Users of all ages should be encouraged to explore all sorts of information, especially information that aids in learning and understanding in matters of schoolwork or employment. The challenge is to do so while (1) remaining focused on why the information is

for Democracy and Technology, stated, "There's a lot about the technology used by the FBI that could be publicly discussed, and deserves to be publicly discussed. This is a hugely important case, because the government says if it can't get what it wants by other means, it will break into your house and plant a device that records everything you type until it gets what it wants."[13]

Young people use keylogging software to find out all sorts of information. With a simple install of a keylogger program, they can learn a parent's password to gain administrative access, credit card information, game cheats, or academic information. In 2005, a 16-year-old high school student from Fort Bend, Texas, was arrested for utilizing a keylogger program. The teen installed the keylogger program and device onto a teacher's computer and was able to capture answers to upcoming tests. The keylogger was installed on the teacher's computer for four days, during which time the student was able to retrieve test answers that he sold to his peers. The teen later confessed to his actions and was reprimanded for such behavior.[14]

being sought, (2) understanding how it relates to responsibilities at hand, and (3) keeping track of how much time is being spent online in relation to the overall amount of time a given project requires. But Internet content can be so tempting—filled with eye-catching Web pages, videos, and pop-up advertisements—it really can be hard to remain focused. Add to this genuinely productive multitasking along with and including instant messages, Facebook updates, and playing online games, it is no wonder that even conscientious students and workers can become distracted when online.

Since it is common for people to enjoy so many features of computing and the Internet in their daily lives, users everywhere, of all ages, and regardless of their student or occupational status, must learn to engage responsibly in online activities. The alternative is that Internet and gaming addiction negatively affects the lives of users and players on psychological, social, and physical levels. The consequences of addictions experienced by addicts are considered direct harms.

While most people can keep online activities on a casual level and not have it impair life functions, for some it can alienate them from real-life activities, damage relationships with families and significant others, contribute to declines in academic or job performance, and cause feelings of withdrawal, anger, depression, and insomnia when not online. Family, friends, classmates, and coworkers of addicts who experience consequences of their addiction suffer indirect harms.

Tertiary harms of addiction are experienced by society at large. The problem has been widely acknowledged in countries such as China and South Korea, which have set legal limits on play time for online games. Games such as MMOGs are designed for maximum playing time in order to make progress and the resulting gold, weapons, and power that comes with achieving higher levels. But this maximum playing time comes with a price for many players. While applying the term "addiction" to these cases may be the subject of debate, the resulting harm from their behavior is not, as evidenced by those who have sought or required mental health intervention as a result of their problems.

Practicing Safe and Responsible Computing

John is a 19-year-old college student who enjoys playing World of Warcraft (WoW) *in his spare time. He has been playing the game for three years now and enjoys having endless amounts of free time while he is at college because he does not have the numerous chores or family activities he did while living at home. John plays WoW any time that he is not in class. He also enjoys grabbing fast food on his way home from class so he can have even more time playing WoW. As a result, his food bill is quite high based on his drive-thru food habit and numerous energy drinks he consumes to stay up into the early hours of the morning. John declined an on-campus job so that he could enjoy many hours of WoW time. To keep up with his gaming, John asks for money from his parents on a weekly basis.*

John, like many other gamers, can become completely entangled in his gaming life so that activities such as working part time, doing schoolwork, or even cooking a meal can seem like time wasted. John's willingness to spend extra money on fast food so

117

that he could spend more time gaming and to continuously ask for money so that he wouldn't need to work illustrate his excessive commitment to World of Warcraft. Becoming completely wrapped up in a video game can cause someone to become in debt and spend erroneously for the sole purpose of keeping up with the life of the video game.

The Internet was developed originally for research and educational purposes. It has evolved into a tool that billions of people can use to stay in touch with friends, find information, and play games. Moderation is an important aspect of engaging in any activity. It is never healthy for people to immerse themselves in something for too long. In the above story, John may or may not need help with his issues. An important first step, however, for anyone who may think they have a problem is to recognize the warning signs.

SIGNS OF ADDICTION—IDENTIFYING AND RECOGNIZING A PROBLEM

Playing a video game or using the Internet for school or personal reasons does not mean one has an addiction. Also, just because someone uses the Internet or plays games for many hours does not mean that he is addicted. Rather, someone who is addicted cannot control the urge to use the Internet or gaming devices and spends excessive time on the addiction to the detriment of other people and things in his life. For example, committed gamers may spend a ton of money on games and play video games for many hours of each day. Those who are truly addicted, however, are also preoccupied with gaming, have experienced other life problems because of it, and they are unable to stop.

In her book *Caught in the Net: How to Recognize the Signs of Internet Addiction—and a Winning Strategy for Recovery*, Kimberly Young lists eight key signs of Internet addiction and suggests that anyone who agrees to five or more of the eight signs within a six-month period should seek professional help.[1] Young developed the signs based on criteria for pathological gambling. She believes the eight signs for potential Internet addiction are:

1. Feeling preoccupied with the Internet (thinking about previous online activity or anticipating the next online session)
2. Feeling the need to use the Internet for increasing amounts of time to achieve satisfaction
3. Making repeated, unsuccessful efforts to control, cut back, or stop Internet use
4. Feeling restless, moody, depressed, or irritable when attempting to cut down or stop Internet use
5. Staying online longer than originally intended
6. Jeopardizing or risking the loss of a significant relationship, job, or educational or career opportunity because of the Internet
7. Lying to family members, therapists, or others to conceal the extent of involvement with the Internet
8. Using the Internet as a way to escape from problems or relieve a dysphoric mood (i.e., feelings of helplessness, guilt, anxiety, and depression)

Spending excessive amounts of money on games and online activities can also be a sign of a problem. Games can be purchased from retail stores and online. They range in price depending on the availability, type, and promotion of the game. It is important to understand the difference between someone who purchases only a few video games and someone who exhibits careless spending habits to keep up with electronic gaming interests.

MENTAL HEALTH INTERVENTION AND TREATMENT

Similar to other challenges one might face, it is important to seek professional help if a person feels he or she cannot keep up with daily responsibilities of life or that he or she is failing to hold positive

Internet addiction is a growing concern in China, for both parents and the government. In 2010, research indicated that over 24 million young Chinese were addicted to the Internet. *(Source: Imaginechina via AP Images)*

relationships as a result of the overuse of computing technologies such as online gaming. By identifying a struggle with balancing activities in life, it becomes possible to seek help in figuring out solutions and get back into a normal routine. Psychologists have studied the area of compulsion and addiction for many years and treatments have evolved to assist patients in recovery. As a result, it is not always necessary to find a psychologist who specifically deals with Internet obsessions because the behavior stems from a larger issue of compulsion that can be addressed by any well-trained mental health professional. Psychiatrists are quite concerned about the welfare of children who spend countless hours playing video games and fail to develop friendships, exercise, or do poorly on schoolwork. Today many school and college counselors are learning more about all kinds of addiction. Increasingly these professionals are helping students with problems they experience online and that may involve addictive behaviors.

PSYCHOLOGICAL TREATMENT

Treatment can involve a number of therapies that often begin with a referral to a mental health provider who specializes in addictions. In an inpatient environment, therapies could include counseling (individually or in group meetings); psychotherapy that includes use of medications to aid in controlling thoughts and behaviors; or cognitive therapy through which patients learn to behave differently, for example, to avoid addictive situations in the first place. Combinations of therapies have shown some effectiveness, as has cognitive behavioral therapy (CBT), a type of cognitive therapy. CBT is an approach that helps patients to take control of their impulses by learning how to cope with their cravings. It involves using new thinking skills to modify their negative behaviors. In the case of compulsive gaming, it often involves learning how to use computers responsibly. This is the biggest difference with treatment for people with other addictions. Alcoholics, for example, often have to avoid alcohol completely. It is difficult for video game addicts to avoid computers since they are such a life necessity.

When patients learn to identify their own triggers, urges, and destructive patterns, they learn strategies to cope with these patterns and not succumb to the compulsion. No matter what the therapy, the aim is to increase *time away* from digital screens, while at the same time increase engagement in other positive behaviors. Of course, the type of therapy depends on the individual. Treatment programs should be individually designed based on the severity of the problem and characteristics of the individual.

Treatment of compulsive gaming can also be considered in the context of addiction to the Internet. Addiction to the Internet has been shown to be associated with other co-occurring disorders such as depression and attention deficit-hyperactivity disorder (ADHD), social phobia, and hostility.[2] It is very possible that playing MMOGs, and potentially playing MMOGs excessively, is driven by similar psychological disorders such as depression and social anxiety. Therefore treatment for compulsive gaming may involve identifying an underlying psychological issue and treating it accordingly.

GAMERS ANONYMOUS GROUPS

Support groups that offer online gamers or others the ability to discuss their feelings can also provide a way to further assist in developing positive and healthy habits to maintain a well-balanced lifestyle. Such support groups are available across the world and in some cases offer online assistance as well. Groups are offered for all ages and are easy to join. For example, the On-Line Gamers Anonymous (OLGA) is a self-help fellowship offered online. OLGA was founded by Liz Woolley in 2002, following the suicide of her son, Shawn, after he became addicted to the computer game *EverQuest*. This group allows its members to share experiences, strengths, and hopes in recovery caused by excessive game play, whether it is on the computer, video, console, or online. Family members and friends can also join in support of someone. OLGA (http://www .olganon.org) employs a 12-step program aimed at helping gamers and their families.

PREVENTING ADDICTION

Preventing all forms of addiction is a huge societal challenge. Millions of people are addicted to a variety of things such as online gaming, gambling, substances, online pornography and various kinds of activities, including certain kinds of behaviors which when engaged in excessively may become unhealthy. Excessive running, for example, may become an addiction for some people. Fortunately several kinds of organizations and other kinds of resources exist to aid society in preventing addiction. These include, but are not limited to, parents and other supervising adults, schools and government agencies, along with health care/ treatment organizations.

Parental Supervision and Positive Adult Role Modeling

It is quite evident that when employing the concept of moderation in any behavior, the chances of harmful side effects caused by excessive use are reduced. Eating too many sweets, staying up too late, or playing outside in the snow for too long can result in

Ben Alexander (*left*), a client of the ReSTART Internet Addiction Recovery Program, works with Gary Simmons in building a chin-up bar in Fall City, Washington, to encourage physical activity. ReSTART is the first addiction program of its kind in the United States. *(Source: AP Photo/Stephen Brashear)*

harmful effects. As a result, it is important that parents and guardians provide positive adult role modeling. Positive adult role modeling involves parents not only teaching children through talking, but by also practicing what they preach. For example, if a father is using the computer to play video games for countless hours late into the night, his children will think it is acceptable for them to follow suit. iKeepSafe (http://www.ikeepsafe.org/) is an online resource that helps parents, educators, and youth to effectively communicate with each other.

The Role of Schools and Government
in Preventing Addictions

Teachers and administrators in schools sometimes do not adequately understand the IT devices that are used by young people and the ways in which they use them. In many cases teachers are just beginning to learn how to use these devices to teach students and understand how students interact with each other through them. Therefore it is hard for teachers to understand some of the dangers and effects of overuse of the Internet and other IT devices and addictive behaviors. It is difficult for them to judge

TRAGEDY AT AN INTERNET ADDICTION CAMP

Deng Senshan was 13 years old when his parents drove him to the Qihang Salvation Training Camp, which opened in rural China in 2009. The camp promised to cure youth from Internet addiction, an issue that had become publicly feared in China. The camp's brochure stated that 80 percent of Chinese youth suffered from the health hazard. Senshan's parents believed he had the ailment also because he was always playing games such as *World of Warcraft* at Internet cafés or on his desktop computer. As a result, his grades dropped and he stopped exercising. Due to his "bad behavior," Deng Senshan's parents paid 7,000 yuan (about $1,000) for one month of treatment at the camp. At the time, China was experiencing a dramatic increase in technology use among its citizens and youth, and the government also feared that it was a threat to their society and therefore needed to be carefully controlled. In this atmosphere of fear, Senshan's parents felt they had no choice but to send him to camp.

Deng Senshan lasted only one day at the camp, which began with a visit to the confinement room. When he refused to "face the wall," he was struck by counselors. A 13-year-old girl who was also at when a student is going "overboard" with the technology they are utilizing.

Government leaders are also finding it to be a great challenge in understanding how IT devices are to be used effectively to promote social computing and learning among children. The need to effectively create laws and govern society in a manner that does not impede on personal freedoms is important, and yet in most cases those that are creating policies do not adequately understand the technology. Therefore it is crucial for young people to take a stand in acting responsibly while using their IT devices and speaking

the camp due to skipping school to chat online said that she heard screams, but that it was normal to hear screams. Later, at about 9 P.M., Senshan and three others were forced to run laps outside the basketball courts, and after about 30 laps, Senshan stumbled and fell. A counselor then dragged him to the side and struck him with the leg of a wooden chair. After an additional beating with a plastic stool, Senshan was dragged to his bunk, screaming, "They're killing me!" He was bleeding from many areas of his face. He was left there for hours before being taken to a hospital where, just 14 hours after arriving at camp, he was pronounced dead.

More than 12 people were jailed as a result of the death, and the camp founder and the claims in its ads were later determined to be frauds. After additional reports of similar experiences at other camps, there was concern in China because the 300 to 400 Internet addiction camps appeared to be unregulated. The parents of Senshan were eventually compensated by the Chinese government, and China's Ministry of Health drafted guidelines for camps, banning physical punishment and use of force.

Afterward Senshan's parents came to a heartbreaking conclusion that he was never addicted in the first place. According to his father, "The Internet was probably his way to vent the pressure on him. We didn't know that then. But we know that now. It wasn't really an addiction. It was his way out of the pressure of being a student."[3]

out on the benefits of these devices within their home, school, and place of employment.

Self regulation and responsibility are important in avoiding a compulsive and addictive routine involving online gaming, shopping, or surfing the Web. Educators, government officials, and community members all play an important role in guiding people to develop positive and healthy behaviors, but individuals have to follow the guides by making smart decisions. Educators spend countless hours interacting with youth, and thus it is important for teachers to inform youth about the harmful aspects of addiction, even in cases of someone being consumed in an online gaming community. By giving examples of warning signs, harmful aspects, and the economic and social burden one might face, educators can help youth take into consideration the need to monitor and regulate their daily activities.

It is also important for the government to sponsor schools and teachers so that they can offer prevention curriculum that specifically includes harmful aspects of the Internet and computing technologies. By offering such sponsorship on a federal level, the government will be making a direct stance about the importance of the issue. Organizations such as Netsmartz (http://www.netsmartz .org) and iKeepSafe offer curriculum and guidance for parents, teachers, and children on how to utilize IT devices in a safe and responsible manner.

Creating Laws and Regulations for Health Care Assistance

Video game addiction is not currently part of the Diagnostic Statistic Manual and medical officials cannot relate video game addiction to that of alcoholism or drug use. It is hard for medical professionals, government officials, and the gaming industry to develop laws that protect consumers from potential side effects of the overuse. Unlike dangerous drugs, a law enforcement officer cannot stop an individual from partaking in playing video games. As a result, it is important for government officials to work effectively with health care professionals and the gaming industry to develop standards and regulations that protect gamers from harmful effects.

Once the American Medical Association recognizes video game addiction as a serious problem, patients suffering from video game addiction and mental health specialists can work together to a greater extent than is currently possible. Furthermore if such addiction is written into a future edition of the DSM, insurance companies can offer compensation for those requesting care at mental health clinics. This will not only assist patients in receiving care for their addiction but also assist families with undue stress as a result of the financial burden of taking care of the individual addicted to video games.[4]

CONCLUSION

The purpose of this book is not to try to solve all the mysteries of technology and addiction. Numerous other books and research by many reputable scientists have not yet been able to do this. Whether it is called Internet addiction (IAD) or problematic Internet use (PIU), there is no question that this is in an issue for an increasing number of people. Still there is some debate about the definition of "Internet addiction" because using the Internet can mean so many things. For example, a person may question whether someone is addicted to the Internet or to activities that are done via the Internet. This includes, but is certainly not limited to, viewing online pornography, shopping, gambling, stock trading, chatting, networking, information searching, and gaming, among other activities. In reality, people can become addicted to all the things that the Internet allows them to do. The Internet is only the vehicle.

It is important to consider that problems related to the Internet are often connected to the interpersonal uses of the Internet. In other words, choices people make about online content and activities they engage in, along with their connections to people online, may be sources of Internet addiction. Interpersonal activities are the reason why many people use social networking sites and play games such as MMOGs. Therefore individuals and families should strive for balance in their lives, which means knowing that there is a time and place for everything, including using the Internet and playing online and electronic games as well as other digital activities. There can be a dark side to technology immersion when taken too far. People should recognize the potential for compulsivity by considering the addictive aspects of technology and within themselves. Kicking the habit can be difficult given the prevalence, exposure, and necessity of information technology today. The first step involves being aware that Web activity and online relationships should not replace "real-life" social connections and experiences. It is important to use the technology responsibly, which means being aware of limits and knowing how important it is to stay in control of one's own behavior.

ENDNOTES

INTRODUCTION

1. Winston Ross, "A World-Wide Woe," *Newsweek*, http://www.newsweek.com/2009/10/07/a-world-wide-woe.html (Accessed August 12, 2011).

CHAPTER 1

1. Deidre O'Connell, "Computer Addiction: One Mother's True Story," Yahoo! Associated Content, http://www.associatedcontent.com/article/21756/computer_addiction_one_mothers_true_pg3.html?cat=9 (Accessed August 12, 2011).

2. Jerald J. Block, "Issues for DSM V: Internet Addiction," *American Journal of Psychiatry*, 165, no. 3 (March 1, 2008): 306–307.

3. Chih-Hung Ko, Gin-Chung Liu, Sigmund Hsiao, Ju-Yu Yen, Ming-Jen Yang, Wei-Chin Lin, Cheng-Fang Yen, and Cheng-Sheng Chen, "Brain Activities Associated with Gaming Urge of Online Gaming Addiction," *Journal of Psychiatric Research*, 43, no. 7 (April 2009): 739–747.

4. Bobby Dobbin, "Texting While Driving: Message Sent from Driver's Phone: Records Show Text Message Exchange around Time of Fatal Crash," ABC News, http://abcnews.go.com/usstory?id=3378025.6 (Accessed July 9, 2008).

5. Science Daily "Video Games Activate Reward Regions of Brain in Men More Than Women," http://www.sciencedaily.com/releases/2008/02/080204140115.htm. (Accessed August 12, 2011).

6. Howard J. Shaffer, et. al. "Toward a Syndrome Model of Addiction: Multiple Expressions, Common Etiology," *Harvard Review of Psychiatry*, 12, no. 6 (November–December 2004): 367–74.

7. Chih-Hung Ko, et.al., "Brain Activities."

8. Fumikio Hoest, Christa L. Watson, Shelli R. Kesler, Keith E. Bettinger, and Allan L. Reiss, "Gender Differences in the Mesocorticolimbic System During Computer Game-Play," *Journal of Psychiatric Research*, 42, no. 4 (March 2008): 253–8.

CHAPTER 2

1. The Criminal Report Daily, "Arizona Teen Sentenced in Father's Senseless Murder," Investigation Discovery, http://blogs.discovery.com/criminal_report/2009/08/arizona-teen-sentenced-in-fathers-senseless-murder.html (Accessed August 12, 2011).

2. Marc Prensky, "Digital Natives, Digital Immigrants," *On the Horizon*, 9, no. 5 (October 2001): 1-6.

3. Samuel C. McQuade and Neel Sampat, "RIT Survey of Internet and at-Risk Behaviors," Report from Rochester Institute of Technology, (2008).

4. Lee Rainee, "The Future of the Internet: Expert Survey Results," Presentation by the Pew Research Center Internet

and American Life Project, San Diego, Calif., 2010.

5. Amanda Lenhart, "Adults and Social Network Websites," Pew Internet Project Data Memo, (2009).

6. WPVI-TV/DT Philadelphia, "Battling Facebook Addiction," ABC Action News, http://abc local.go.com/wpvi/story?section =news/special_reports&id= 7251938 (Accessed August 12, 2011).

CHAPTER 3

1. Mike Smith, "Couple Starves Real Child While Raising Virtual One," Yahoo! Games, http:// videogames.yahoo.com/events/ plugged-in/couple-starves-real-child-while-raising-virtual-one/ 1392152 (Accessed August 12, 2011).

2. Lydia Sung, "Young Boy Commits Suicide over Video Games," Ne-oseeker, http://www.neoseeker .com/news/10794-young-boy-commits-suicide-over-video-games/ (Accessed August 12, 2011).

3. Amanda Lenhart, Joseph Kahne, Ellen Middaugh, Alexandra Rankin Macgill, Chris Evans, Jessica Vitak, "Teens, Video Games, and Civics," Pew Internet and American Life Project, (2008).

4. Ibid.

5. Amanda Lenhart and Alexandra Rankin Macgill, "Pew Internet Project Data Memo," Pew Internet and American Life Project, (2008).

6. Entertainment Software Rating Board (ESRB), "Games Rating and Descriptor Guide," http://

www.esrb.org/ratings/ratings_ guide.jsp (Accessed August 12, 2011).

7. Amanda Lenhart, "Teens, Video Games, and Civics."

8. Ibid.

9. Richard Ryan, C. Scott Rigby, and Andrew Pryzbylski, "The Motivational Pull of Video Games: A Self Determination Theory Approach," *Motivation and Emotion,* 30, no. 4 (2006): 344–360.

10. The Voice of Internet Gaming (VOIG), http://www.voig.com (Accessed October 8, 2010).

11. M.D. Griffiths, M.N. Davies, and D. Chappell, "Breaking the Stereotype: The Case of Online Gaming," *CyberPsychology & Behavior,* 6, no. 1 (2004): 6 N1.

12. Lindsey Tanner, "Is Video-Game Addiction a Mental Disorder?," Games on MSNBC.com, http://www.msnbc.msn.com/ id/19354827/ (Accessed August 12, 2011).

13. K. Chak and L. Leung, "Shyness and Locus of Control as Predictors of Internet Addiction and Internet Use," *CyberPsychology & Behavior,* 7, no. 5 (2004): 559–570.

14. Shang Hwa Hsu, Ming-Hui Wen, and Muh-Cherng Wu, "Exploring User Experiences as Predictors of MMORPG Addiction," *Computers & Education,* 53, no. 3 (2009): 990–999.

15. Aaron Dunlap, "Gamer Commits Suicide Media Misreports," Game Bump, http://www.game bump.com/go/gamer_commits _suicide_media_misreports (Accessed August 12, 2011).

16. Scott Caplan, Dmitri Williams, and Nick Yee, "Problematic

Internet Use and Psychosocial Well-Being Among MMO Players," *Computers in Human Behavior*, 25, no. 6 (November 2009), 1312–1319.

17. Richard Ryan, "Cause and Impact of Video Games Addiction," NRDI.com, http://ndri.com/article/cause_and_impact_of_video_games_addiction_-211.html (Accessed July 11, 2010).

CHAPTER 4

1. Emily Verbeke and Karin Dittrick-Nathan, "Student Gambling," *Principal Leadership* (2007): 12–15.

2. National Research Council, *Pathological Gambling: A Critical Review.* (Washington D.C.: National Academy Press, 1997).

3. Ibid.

4. Robert J. Williams and Robert T. Wood, "Internet Gambling: a Comprehensive Review and Synthesis of the Literature," *Report Prepared for the Ontario Problem Gambling Research Centre, Guelph, Ontario, Canada,* (2007), http://www.gamblingresearch.org/content/research.php?appid=3074 (Accessed August 12, 2011).

5. R. Labrie, D. LaPlante, S. Nelson, A. Schumann, and H. Shaffer, "Assessing the Playing Field: A Prospective Longitudinal Study of Internet Sports Gambling Behavior," *Journal of Gambling Studies,* 23, no. 3 (2007): 347–362.

6. Science Daily, "Estimated 750,000 Problem Gamblers among America's Youth," http://www.sciencedaily.com/releases/2008/05/080506

163918.htm (Accessed August 12, 2011).

7. Ibid., Williams and Wood

8. Douglas Gentile, "Pathological Video Game Use among Youth Ages 8–10," *Psychological Science,* 20, no. 5 (2008): 1–9.

9. Ibid., Williams and Wood

CHAPTER 5

1. Amanda Lenhart, Rich Ling, Scott Campbell, and Kristen Purcell, "Teens and Mobile Phones," Pew Internet and American Life Project, 2010.

2. Aaron Smith, "Mobile Access 2010," Pew Internet and American Life Project, 2010.

3. Governors Highway Safety Association, "Cell Phone and Texting Laws," State Laws & Funding, http://www.ghsa.org/html/stateinfo/laws/cellphone_laws.html (Accessed August 12, 2011).

4. Bob Tedeschi, "A Gimmick Becomes a Real Trend," *New York Times,* http://www.nytimes.com/2007/11/26/technology/26ecom.html?_r=2&oref=slogin (Accessed August 12, 2011).

5. Business Wire, "On Black Friday Leading Retail Web Sites Slow Way Down, Reports Keynote Systems," PR-Inside.com, http://www.pr-inside.com/on-black-friday-leading-retail-web-r1605481.htm (Accessed August 12, 2011).

6. Business Journals Incorporated, "Minors in WA Buy Alcohol on Internet," *Entrepreneur,* http://www.entrepreneur.com/tradejournals/article/122262559.html (Accessed August 12, 2011).

7. Parents Television Council, "Facts and TV Statistics: 'It's Just Harmless Entertainment' Oh Really?" http://www.parentstv.org/ptc/facts/mediafacts.asp (Accessed August 12, 2011).

8. Dave N. Greenfield, "The Net Effect: Internet Addiction and Compulsive Internet Use," The Center for Internet and Technology Addiction, http://www.virtual-addiction.com (Accessed August 12, 2011).

CHAPTER 6

1. MetroLyrics, "American Idol's Australian Cyber-stalker Sent to Jail," http://www.metrolyrics.com/2009-american-idoloss-australian-cyber-stalker-sent-to-jail-news.html (Accessed August 12, 2011).

2. Lester Haines, "Online Gamer Stabbed Over 'Stolen' Cyber-sword," Out-Law.com, http://www.outlaw.com/page-5474 (Accessed August 12, 2011).

3. BBC News, "Chinese Gamer Sentenced to Life," http://news.bbc.co.uk/1/hi/technology/4072704.stm (Accessed August 12, 2011).

4. American Academy of Sleep Medicine, "Excessive Gaming Associated with Poor Sleep Hygiene and Increased Sleepiness," Science Daily, http://www.sciencedaily.com/releases/2009/06/090608071802.htm (Accessed August 12, 2011).

5. Nintendo, "Nintendo GameCube Health & Safety Precautions Manual–English," http://www.nintendo.com/consumer/manuals/precautions_gcn_

english.jsp (Accessed August 12, 2011).

6. Justin Fielding, "Chinese Gamer Dies From Exhaustion!" Tech-Republic, http://blogs.techrepublic.com.com/networking/?p=340 (Accessed August 12, 2011).

7. The Earth Times, "Vietnamese boy, 13, Kills Woman for Money to Play Video Games," http://www.earthtimes.org/articles/show/144906.html (Accessed July 21, 2011).

8. Robert Half International, "Impaired Functioning at Work: Surf's Up! Is Productivity down?", Press Release, Robert Half International, (1996).

9. J.R. Meloy, "The Psychology of Stalking," The Psychology of Stalking: Clinical and Forensic Perspectives, (San Diego, Calif.: Academic Press, 1998).

10. Federal Trade Commission, "Fighting Back Against Identity Theft," http://www.ftc.gov/bcp/edu/microsites/idtheft/consumers/about-identity-theft.html (Accessed August 12, 2011).

11. Aaron Emigh, "Online Identity Theft: Phishing Technology, Chokepoints and Countermeasures," Radix Labs, (2005): 1–58.

12. John Leyden, "Mafia Trial to Test FBI Spying Tactics," The Register, http://www.theregister.co.uk/2000/12/06/mafia_trial_to_test_fbi/ (Accessed August 12, 2011).

13. George A. Chidi, "FBI Wants to Keep Digital Snooping Secret: Keystroke-Recorder Used in Mob Case is a Matter of National Security, Government Says," Guyana Under Siege, http://www.guyanaundersiege.com/

Single%20Pages/Privacy.htm (Accessed August 12, 2011).

14. The Internet Patrol, "Teen Steals Information with Keylogger," http://www.theinternetpatrol .com/teen-steals-exam-answers-with-key-logger/ (Accessed August 12, 2011).

CHAPTER 7

1. Kimberly Young, *Caught in the Net: How to Recognize the Signs of Internet Addiction—and a Winning Strategy for Recovery.* (New York: John Wiley & Sons, 1998).

2. J.Y. Yen, C.F.Yen, and C.S. Chen, "The Association Between Adult ADHD Symptoms and Internet Addiction Among College Students: the Gender Difference," *CyberPsychology & Behavior,* 12, no. 2 (April 2009): 187–191.

3. Christopher S. Stewart, "Obsessed with the Internet: a Tale from China," Wired.com, February 2010, http://www .wired.com/magazine/2010/01/ ff_internetaddiction/ (Accessed August 12, 2011).

4. Chih-Hung Ko, et. al., "Brain Activities."

BIBLIOGRAPHY

Acohido, Byron, and Jon Swartz. "Malicious-Software Spreaders Get Sneakier, More Prevalent," *USA Today*. Available online. URL: http://www.usatoday.com/tech/news/computersecurity/infotheft/2006-04-23-bot-herders_x.htm. Posted April 23, 2006.

Akdeniz, Yaman. "Controlling Illegal and Harmful Content on the Internet." *Crime and the Internet*. London: Routledge, 2001.

American Psychiatric Association. *Diagnostic and Statistical Manual of Mental Disorders*, 4th ed. Washington, D.C.: American Psychiatric Association, 1994.

Armour, Nancy. "Blogs, Photo Sites Give Everyone a Peek at Athletes' Lives," *Charleston Gazette*. Available online. URL: http://www.highbeam.com/doc/1P2-13920652.html. Posted on May 27, 2006.

Associated Press. "Colleges Reminding Freshmen About Internet Dangers," *USA Today*. Available online. URL: http://www.usatoday.com/tech/news/internetprivacy/2006-07-25-university-net-warning_x.htm. Posted July 25, 2006.

———. "Girl, 12, Charged with Distributing Nude Pic of Classmate," FOX News. Available online. URL: http://www.foxnews.com/story/0,2933,370987,00.html. Posted June 24, 2008.

———. "Seller of AOL Data Is Sentenced," *New York Times*. Available online. URL: http://www.nytimes.com/2005/08/18/technology/18spam.html?pagewanted=print. Posted August 18, 2005.

———. "Study: Rising Number of Kids Exposed to Online Porn," FOX News. Available online. URL: http://www.foxnews.com/story/0,2933,250247,00.html. Posted February 5, 2007.

Audi, Tamara. "U.S. Deals Blow to Online-Poker Players," *Wall Street Journal*. Available online. URL: http://online.wsj.com/article_email/SB124459561862800591-lMyQjAxMDI5NDE0MDUxOTA1Wj.html. Posted June 10, 2009.

Baig, Edward. "Symantec Service Helps Parents Keep a Cyber Eye on the Kids," *USA Today*. Available online. URL: http://www.usatoday .com/tech/columnist/edwardbaig/2009-04-22-symantec-norton-kids-parents_N.htm. Posted April 23, 2009.

Baigorri, Manuel. "Internet Addiction Growing around the World," UPI.com. Available online. URL: http://www.upi.com/Top_News/ Special/2008/07/30/Analysis-Internet-addiction-growing/UPI-94571217432254/. Posted July 30, 2008.

Barry, Dan. "A Boy the Bullies Love to Beat Up, Repeatedly," *New York Times*. Available online. URL: http://www.nytimes.com/ 2008/03/24/us/24land.html?pagewanted=1. Posted March 24, 2008.

Becker, David. "Is Microsoft Using 'Halo 2' to Thwart Xbox Hackers?" CNET.com. Available online. URL: http://news .cnet.com/Is-Microsoft-using-Halo-2-to-thwart-Xbox-hackers/ 2100-1043_3-5449160.html. Posted November 12, 2004.

Brunker, Mike. "Is Anything Taboo in 'Toon Porn'? Weighing the Moral and Legal Questions," MSNBC.com. Available online. URL: http://www.msnbc.msn.com/id/6282737/ns/news-internet_ underground/t/anything-taboo-toon-porn/. Posted October 22, 2004.

———. "'Toon Porn' Pushes Erotic Envelope Online: Adult Animation Booming on Web, Spreading to Mainstream Media," MSNBC.com. Available online. URL: http://www.msnbc.msn.com/ id/6227619/ns/news-internet_underground/t/toon-porn-pushes-erotic-envelope-online/. Posted October 19, 2004.

Burgess-Proctor, Amanda, J. Patchin, and S. Hinduja. *Female Crime Victims: Reality Reconsidered*. Edited by Vanessa Garcia and Janice Clifford. Upper Saddle River, N.J.: Prentice Hall, 2008.

Casey, Eoghan. *Digital Evidence and Computer Crime.*, 2d ed. Waltham, Mass.: Academic Press, 2004.

Center, National White Collar Crime. "IFCC 2002 Internet Fraud Report." Washington, D.C.: National White Collar Crime Center,

2003. Available online. URL: http://www.ic3.gov/media/annual report/2002_IFCCReport.pdf. Accessed August 12, 2011.

Cha, Ariana Eunjung. "In China, Stern Treatment for Young Internet 'Addicts,'" *Washington Post.* Available online. URL: http://www.washingtonpost.com/wp-dyn/content/article/2007/02/21/AR2007022102094.html.Accessed August 12, 2011.

Charles Katz v. United States, 389 US 347 (1967).

Chatterjee, Bela Bonita. "Last of the Rainmacs: Thinking About Pornography in Cyberspace." *Crime and the Internet.* London: Routledge, 2001.

Cheng, Jacqui. "Craigslist Gives in, Will Shut Down Erotic Services Section," Ars Technica. Available online. URL: http://arstechnica.com/tech-policy/news/2009/05/craigslist-gives-in-will-shut-down-erotic-services-section.ars. Accessed August 12, 2011.

———. "Game Server Admins Arrested for Chinese DNS Attacks," Ars Technica. Available online. URL: http://arstechnica.com/web/news/2009/08/game-server-admins-arrested-for-chinese-dns-attacks.ars. Accessed August 12, 2011.

Clark, Noelene. "Internet Sex-Offender Bill Draws Praise, Ire," Scripps Howard Foundation Wire. Available online. URL: http://www.shfwire.com/node/4684. Accessed August 12, 2011.

Collison, Michele. "Survey at Rutgers Suggests That Cheating May Be on the Rise at Large Universities." *Chronicle of Higher Education* 37, no. 8 (1990): A31.

Dabrowski, Wojtek. "Unable to Unplug, Tech Addicts May Sue, Researcher Says: Could Gadgets Like Blackberries and Cell Phones Ring up Lawsuits?" MacDork. Available online. URL: http://www.macdork.com/2006/08/30/unable-to-unplug-tech-addicts-may-sue-researcher-says/. Accessed August 12, 2011.

Davis, Stephen F., Cathy Grover, A., Angela H. Becker, and Loretta N McGregor. "Academic Dishonesty: Prevalence, Determinants, Techniques, and Punishments." *Teaching of Psychology* 19, no. 1 (1992): 16–20.

Denning, Dorothy E, and William E. Baugh, eds. *Encryption and Evolving Technologies as Tools of Organized Crime and Terrorism.* Washington, D.C.: National Strategy Information Center, U.S. Working Group on Organized Crime (WGOC), 1997.

Dibbell, Julian. "Serfing the Web: Black Snow Interactive and the World's First Virtual Sweat Shop," Julian Dibbell.com. Available online. URL: http://www.juliandibbell.com/texts/blacksnow.html. Accessed August 12, 2011.

———. "The Unreal Estate Boom," Wired.com. Available online. URL: http://www.wired.com/wired/archive/11.01/gaming.html. Accessed August 12, 2011.

Earley, P., ed. *Super Casino: Inside the "New" Las Vegas.* New York: Bantam Books, 2000.

Electronic Arts, Inc. "EA Game Authorization Management." Available online. URL: http://activate.ea.com/deauthorize/. Accessed August 12, 2011.

Electronic Frontier Foundation. Available online. URL: http://www .eff.org. Accessed August 12, 2011.

Entertainment Software Rating Board. "Game Ratings & Descriptor Guide." Available online. URL: http://www.esrb.org/ ratings/ratings_guide.jsp. Accessed August 12, 2011.

Erard, Michael. "The Ivy-Covered Console," *New York Times.* Available online. URL: http://www.nytimes.com/2004/02/26/technology /the-ivy-covered-console.html. Accessed August 12, 2011.

eSchool Staff and Wire Reports. "COPA Dies Quietly in Supreme Court: 10-Year-Old Online Pornography Law Will Never Take Effect," eSchool News. Available online. URL: http://www.eschool news.com/2009/01/22/copa-dies-quietly-in-supreme-court/. Accessed August 12, 2011.

Farache, Emily. "'Star Trek' Stalker Sentenced," E Online, *Chelsea Lately.* Available online. URL: http://www.eonline.com/on/shows/ chelsea/chelseaness/b41556_star_trek_stalker_sentenced.html. Accessed August 12, 2011.

Feldman, Curt. "Banned Sims Blogger Bites Back," GameSpot. Available online. URL: http://www.gamespot.com/news/6085767/ qanda-banned-sims-blogger-bites-back. Accessed August 12, 2011.

Finn, Jerry. "A Survey of Online Harassment at a University Campus." *Journal of Interpersonal Violence* 19 (2004): 468–83.

Foster, Andrea L. "New Systems Keep a Close Eye on Online Students at Home," *The Chronicle of Higher Education*. Available online. URL: http://chronicle.com/article/New-Systems-Keep-a-Close-Eye/22559. Accessed August 12, 2011.

Gill, M. S. "Cybercops Take a Byte out of Computer Crime." *Smithsonian* (May 1997): 114–24.

Gluck, Caroline. "South Korea's Gaming Addicts," BBC News. Available online. URL: http://news.bbc.co.uk/2/hi/asia-pacific/2499957. stm. Accessed August 12, 2011.

Gopher, D., and E. Donchin. *Workload: An Examination of the Concept*. New York: John Wiley, 1986.

Gram, Dave. "Teens Accused of 'Sexting' May Not Face Child Porn Charges in Vermont," CNS News.com. Available online. URL: http://www.cnsnews.com/node/46587. Accessed August 12, 2011.

Hoffman, Donna L., and Thomas P. Novak. "A Detailed Analysis of the Conceptual, Logical and Methodological Flaws in the Article: 'Marketing Pornography on the Information Superhighway,'" Content-analysis.de. Available online. URL: http://www .content-analysis.de/2008/01/16/detailed-analysis-of-the-concep tual-logical-and-methodological-flaws-in-the-article-marketing-pornography-on-the-information-superhighway.html. Accessed August 12, 2011.

Hollinger, Richard C., and L. Lanza-Kaduce. "Academic Dishonesty and Perceived Effectiveness of Countermeasures: An Empircal Survey of College Cheating." *NASPA Journal 33*, no. 4 (1996): 292–306.

Hospers, J. "The Best Action Is the One with the Best Consequences." *Computers, Ethics and Society*. New York: Oxford University Press, 2003.

Howe, Jeff. "The Shadow Internet," Wired.com. Available online. URL: http://www.wired.com/wired/archive/13.01/topsite.html. Accessed August 12, 2011.

Hughes, Donna M. "The Impact of the Use of New Communications and Information Technologies on Trafficking in Human Beings for Sexual Exploitation: A Study of the Users," Council of Europe. Available online. URL: http://www.coe.int/t/dghl/monitoring/ trafficking/docs/activities/EGSNT2002-9rev_en.asp. Accessed August 12, 2011.

———. "Sexual Exploitation and the Internet in Cambodia." *Journal of Sexual Aggression* 6, no. 1–2 (2003): 1–23.

Irvine, Martha. "Porn Charges for 'Sexting' Stir Debate: At Issue: Should Teens Who Send Racy Cell-Phone Pictures Be Branded as Sex Offenders?" MSNBC.com. Available online. URL: http:// www.msnbc.msn.com/id/29017808/ns/technology_and_science tech_and_gadgets/t/porn-charges-sexting-stir-debate/. Accessed August 12, 2011.

Jackel, Donna. "Experts Aim to Boost Child Safety." *Democrat and Chronicle*, August 11, 2005, 3B-4B, Rochester, New York.

James, Stuart H., and Jon J. Nordby, eds. *Forensic Science*. Boca Raton, Fla.: CRC Press, 2003.

Ji-eun, Seo. "Man Arrested for Knocking Out Game Rating Board Site," *Korea JoongAng Daily*. Available online. URL: http://joon gangdaily.joins.com/article/view.asp?aid=2907243. Accessed August 12, 2011.

Kanamine, L. "Gamblers Stake out the 'Net," *USA Today*, November 17, 1995, 1A–2A.

Kerr, Gail. " Honor Code Could Boost Collegiate Integrity." *The Tennessean*, November 17, 2004.

Kintisch, Eli. "Scientific Misconduct: Researcher Faces Prison for Fraud in NIH Grant Applications and Papers." *Science* 307, no. 5717 (2005): 1851.

Kohn, David. "Addicted: Suicide over EverQuest?" 48 Hours. Available online. URL: http://www.cbsnews.com/stories/2002/10/17/48hours/main525965.shtml. Posted February 11, 2009.

Korda, Martin. "The Net's Sleuths." *Guardian Unlimited.* July 15, 2004.

Kruger, R. "Discussing Cyber Ethics with Students Is Critical." *The Social Studies 94*, no. 4 (2003): 188–89.

Levy, S., ed. *Hackers: Heroes of the Computer Revolution.* New York: Doubleday, 1984.

Macgill, Alexandria. "Parent and Teenager Internet Use." Pew Internet and American Life Project (2007): 1–11.

McCafferty, Dennis. "Organized Cyber-Crime." Available online. URL: http://www.thewhir.com/features/organize-cybercrime.cfm. Posted September 1, 2004.

McCarthy, Dave. "A History of Gaming in Nine Influential Genres That Shaped the Industry through the Ages," IGN. Available online. URL: http://retro.ign.com/articles/964/964847p1.html. Accessed August 12, 2011.

McCullagh, Declan. "Police Blotter: Teens Prosecuted for Racy Photos," CNET News. Available online. URL: http://news.cnet.com/Police-blotter-Teens-prosecuted-for-racy-photos/2100-1030_3-6157857.html. Accessed August 12, 2011.

McCullagh, Declan, and Anne Broache. "Congress and Tech: Little to Show," CNET News. Available online. URL: http://news.cnet.com/Congress-and-tech-Little-to-show/2100-1030_3-6142709.html. Accessed August 12, 2011.

McMillan, Robert. "Internet Sieges Can Cost Businesses a Bundle." *ComputerWorld.* Available online. URL: http://www

.computerworld.com/s/article/104168/Internet_sieges_can_cost_businesses_a_bundle. Accessed August 12, 2011.

McQuade, Samuel. C., and Chris Schreck. "Correlates of High Tech Crime Victimization." Presented at the conference of the Midwest Criminal Justice Association, Chicago, Ill. September 20, 2005.

McQuade, Samuel C., and Nathan Fisk. "High Tech Adolescent Offending and Victimization: Towards a New Paradigm for Crime and Deviancy Research." Presented at the National Institute of Justice Conference, Arlington, Va. July 23, 2007.

———. "Cyber Bullying: Preliminary Findings and Early-Age Profiles." Presented at the Monroe County Cyber Bullying Conference, Monroe Community College, Rochester, N.Y.: October 1, 2007.

———Cybercrime: New Conundrums and Challenges in the Paradigm of Evolving Criminality. New York: Oxford University Press, 2008.

———. "IT-Enabled Offending and Victimization By and Among RIT Students: Implications for Student Services, Education and Training." Presented for the Student Affairs Division at the Rochester Institute of Technology, August 17, 2005

———, ed. Monitoring Technologies. In the Encyclopedia of Science, Technology, and Ethics. New York: Macmillan Reference USA, 2005.

———. "Research Needs for Computer Crime." National Institute of Justice, Available online. URL: http://www.crime-research.org/library/introduction.htm. Accessed May 26, 2006.

———. "We Must Educate Young People About Cybercrime before They Start College." Chronicle of Higher Education, January 5, 2007.

McQuade, Samuel C. "Expert Outlines Strategies for Fighting Cybercrime." RIT: The University Magazine, 2005.

———. "High-Tech Abuse and Crime on College and University Campuses: Evolving Forms of Victimization, Offending, and Their Interplay in Higher Education." Chapter 15 in, Bonnie Fisher and John Sloan, eds., *Campus Crime: Legal, Social and Policy Perspectives*, 2nd ed., Springfield, Ill.: Charles C Thomas, 2007.

———. "Technology-Enabled Crime, Policing and Security." *Journal of Technology Studies* 33, no. 1 (2005): 32–42.

McQuade, Samuel C., and Tom Castellano. "Computer Aided Crime and Misbehavior among a Student Population: An Empirical Examination of Patterns, Correlates, and Possible Causes." November 17, 2004.

McQuade, Samuel C., and Neel Sampat. "RIT Survey of Internet and At-Risk Behaviors." Rochester, N.Y.: Rochester Institute of Technology, 2008.

MegaGames. "Vietnamese Boy, 13, Kills Woman for Money to Play Video Games," MegaGames.com. Available online. URL: http://www.megagames.com/news/vietnamese-kid-kills-woman-play-online?tab=description. Accessed August 12, 2011.

Miller, Stanley A. II. "Death of a Game Addict." *Milwaukee Journal Sentinel*. Available online. URL: http://www.free republic.com/focus/chat/658054/posts. Accessed August 12, 2011.

Musil, Steven. "Study: Video Game Play May Improve Eyesight," CNET News. Available online. URL: http://news.cnet.com/8301-10797_3-10206764-235.html?tag=newsEditorsPicksArea.0. Accessed August 12, 2011.

Musto, David F. "Historical Perspectives." *Substance Abuse: A Comprehensive Textbook*. London: Williams and Wilkins, 1997.

National Academies of Science. "Youth, Pornography and the Internet." Washington, D.C.: National Academy Press, 2002.

National Research Council. *Pathological Gambling: A Critical Review*. Washington, D.C.: National Academy Press, 1999.

New Yorker Magazine. "Just Click No." Psycom.net. Available online. URL: http://www.psycom.net/iasg.html. Accessed August 12, 2011.

New York Times. "Vague Cyberbullying Law," *New York Times.* Available online. URL: http://www.nytimes.com/2009/09/08/ opinion/08tue2.html?emc=eta1. Accessed August 12, 2011.

Newsday. "U.S. Law on Web Porn Is Blocked." *Democrat & Chronicle*, Rochester, N.Y., June 30, 2004.

Nichols, Laura, and Richard Nicki. "Development of a Psychometrically Sound Internet Addiction Scale: A Preliminary Step." *Psychology of Addictive Behaviors* 18, no. 4 (2004): 381–84.

Nintendo. "Nintendo GameCube Health & Safety Precautions Manual – English." Available online. URL: http://www.nintendo.com/ consumer/manuals/precautions_gcn_english.jsp. Accessed August 12, 2011.

Nordland, R., and J. Bartholet. "The Web's Dark Secret." *Newsweek* (March 19, 2001): 44–51.

Parker, Donn B., ed. *Crime by Computer.* New York: Charles Scribner's Sons, 1976.

Parkin, Simon. "Triple Rock: Famous or *inFamous*? Morality and Choice in Sucker Punch's Ps3 Debut," Offworld. Available online. URL: http://offworld.boingboing.net/2009/05/29/triple-rock-famous-or-infamous.html. Accessed August 12, 2011.

Peterson, Dane K. "Computer Ethics: The Influence of Guidelines and Universal Moral Beliefs." *Information Technology & People* 15, no. 4 (2002): 346–61.

Prabhu, Maya. " Students Help Program Science Computer Game," eSchool News. Available online. URL: http://www.eschoolnews .com/2009/08/06/students-help-program-science-computer-game/?ast=17. Accessed August 12, 2011.

———. "Gaming Is the Future of Classroom Instruction: FETC 'Eye Opening' Keynote Speaker Jim Brazell Stresses the Importance That Gaming Will Soon Have in K-12 Classrooms," eSchool News. Available online. URL: http://www.eschoolnews.com/2009/01/24/

gaming-is-the-future-of-classroom-instruction/. Accessed August 12, 2011.

Princeton Survey Research Associates International. "Cyberbullying and Online Teens," Philadelphia: Pew Research Center, 2007. http://www.pewinternet.org/pdfs/PIP%20Cyberbullying%20 Memo.pdf. Accessed August 12, 2011.

Rachels, J. "The Best Action Is the One in Accord with Universal Rules." *Computers, Ethics and Society*. Edited by David M. Ermann and Michele S. Shauf. New York: Oxford University Press, 2003.

Rainey, Richard. "Groups Assail 'Most Violent' Video Games, Industry Rating System," *Los Angeles Times*. Available online. URL: http://articles.latimes.com/2004/nov/24/nation/na-games24. Accessed August 12, 2011.

Read, Brock. "Piracy and Copyright: An Ethics Lesson." *Chronicle of Higher Education*, 2006.

———. "Wired for Cheating: Some Professors Go Beyond Honor Codes to Stop Misuse of Electronic Devices." *Chronicle of Higher Education*, 2004.

Reuters. "Video-Game Sales Overtaking Music," MSN.com. Available online. URL: http://articles.moneycentral.msn.com/Investing/ Extra/VideoGameSalesOvertakingMusic.aspx. Accessed August 12, 2011.

Rimm, Martin. "Marketing Pornography on the Information Superhighway." *Georgetown Law Review* 83: 1849–934.

Rogers, D. "Video Is on a Roll at Jails." *Law Enforcement Technology* (June 2002): 16–22.

Rommelmann, Nancy. "Anatomy of a Child Pornographer: What Happens When Adults Catch Teenagers 'Sexting' Photos of Each Other? The Death of Common Sense," Reason.com. Available online. URL: http://www.reason.com/news/show/133863.html. Accessed August 12, 2011.

Sanchez, Julian. "Parents Fight Child Porn Threats Against 'Sexting' Teens," Ars Technica. Available online. URL: http://

arstechnica.com/tech-policy/news/2009/03/parents-fight-child-porn-threats-against-sexting-teens.ars. Accessed August 12, 2011.

Schaef, A.W., and D. Fassel, eds. *The Addictive Organization*. San Francisco: Harper & Row, 1990.

Schwankert, Steven. "AOL Spammer Pleads Guilty." *PC World*. Available online. URL: http://www.pcworld.com/article/132808/aol_spammer_pleads_guilty.html. Posted June 12, 2007.

Science Daily. "Teenagers' Use of Cell Phones after Bedtime Contributes to Poor Sleep." Available online. URL: http://www.sciencedaily.com/releases/2007/09/070901073641.htm. Posted September 3, 2007.

Shachtman, Noah. "Shoot 'Em Up and Join the Army," Wired.com. Available online. URL: http://www.wired.com/gaming/gaming reviews/news/2002/07/53663. Accessed August 12, 2011.

Shaffer, Howard J., Matthew N. Hall, and Joni Vander Bilt. "Computer Addiction: A Critical Consideration." *American Journal of Orthopsychiatry* 70, no. 2 (2000): 162–68.

Shot, Live. "Real Time, Online, Hunting and Shooting Experience." Available online. URL: http://live-shot.com/howitworks.shtml. Accessed November 23, 2004.

Shukovsky, Paul. "Blaster Worm Attacker Gets 18 Months," *Seattle Post Intelliger*. Available online. URL: http://www.seattlepi.com/local/article/Blaster-worm-attacker-gets-18-months-1165231.php. Accessed August 12, 2011.

Snyder, R. J. "Gambling Swindles and Victims." *Journal of Gambling Behavior 2*, no. 1 (1986): 50–57.

Spiegel Online. "School Shooting in Winnenden: Flags in Germany Are Flying at Half-Mast," *Spiegel*. Available online. URL: http://www.spiegel.de/international/germany/0,1518,612940,00.html. Accessed August 12, 2011.

Stambaugh, Hollis, David Beaupre, David J. Icove, Richard Baker, Wayne Cassaday, and Wayne P. Williams. "State and Local Law

Enforcement Needs to Combat Electronic Crime." Washington, D.C.: U.S. Department of Justice, 2000.

Stansbury, Meris "Students Say Using Tech to Cheat Isn't Cheating: New Poll Reveals Students Use Cell Phones, Internet to Cheat; Parents Are Unaware," eSchool News. Available online. URL: http://www.eschoolnews.com/2009/06/18/students-say-using-tech-to-cheat-isnt-cheating/. Accessed August 12, 2011.

Tavani, H. T. "The Uniqueness Debate in Computer Ethics." *Ethics and Information Technology 4*, no. 1 (2002): 37–54.

Terdiman, Daniel. "Tough Task: Designing a Game About Your 'First Time,'" CNN.com. Available online. URL: http://www.cnn.com/2009/TECH/03/27/videogame.losing.virginity/index.html. Accessed August 12, 2011.

Turley, Jonathan. "Bullying's Day in Court from Hall Monitors to Personal Injury Lawyers: Parents Send a Message by Forcing Bullies from the Schoolhouse to the Courthouse," *USA Today*. Available online. URL: http://abcnews.go.com/TheLaw/story?id=5378214&page=1. Accessed August 12, 2011.

Underwood, Barbara B. "Reply Brief for Writ of Certiorari to John Ashcroft, Attorney General of the United States, Petitioner v. American Civil Liberties Union, et al." Washington, D.C.: U.S. Department of Justice, 2001.

Unruh, Bob. "What You Don't Know About 'Sexting' Can Hurt: New Report Says Images Remain on Online Forever," WorldNetDaily. Available online. URL: http://www.wnd.com/index.php?fa=PAGE.view&pageId=95039. Accessed August 12, 2011.

United States Code. Statute 2258a: Reporting Requirements of Electronic Communication Service Providers and Remote Computing Service Providers.

U.S. House of Representatives Committee on Energy and Commerce. *Sexual Exploitation of Children over the Internet: What Parents, Kids and Congress Need to Know About Child Predators*, April 4, 2006.

U.S. Immigration and Customs Enforcement. "Wisconsin Man Gets 10 Years in Prison for Arranging Sex with 8-Year-Old Girl: Made Online Arrangements for Colorado Mother to Bring Daughter to Kenosha for Sex," ICE.gov. Available online. URL: http://www.ice .gov/news/releases/0803/080310milwaukee.htm. Accessed August 12, 2011.

U.S. Secret Service and U.S. Department of Education. "The Final Report and Findings of the Safe School Initiative: Implications for the Prevention of School Attacks in the United States." Washington, D.C.: Government Printing Office, 2002.

Vaugeois, Pierre. "Cyberaddiction: Fundamentals and Perspectives." Montreal, Canada: Centre quebecois de lutte aux dependances, 2006.

Wall, David S. "Son of Spam: Crime Convergence in the Information Age." Presented at the Annual Conference of the American Society of Criminology, Nashville, Tenn., February 18, 2004.

Warner, Bernhard. "Net Crime Gangs Hit Gambling Sites." ISN Net. Available online. URL: http://lists.jammed.com/ISN/2004/01/0092. html. Accessed August 12, 2011.

WHAM TV Channel 13. "Need to Regulate E-Cigarette Debated." Available online. URL: http://www.13wham.com/news/local/story/ Bill-Would-Ban-E-Cigarettes-Until-FDA-Action/bIXhBdlss0W jejo2qhtVkg.cspx. Accessed August 12, 2011.

Wolak, Janis, Kimberly J. Mitchell, and David Finkelhor. "Internet Sex Crimes against Minors: The Response of Law Enforcement." Washington, D.C.: National Center for Missing & Exploited Children, 2003.

 **FURTHER RESOURCES**

BOOKS

Clark, Neils and P. Shavaun Scott. *Game Addiction: The Experience and the Effects.* Jefferson, Jefferson, N.C.: McFarland & Company, 2009.

How video games affect the lives of millions of gamers.

Reith, Gerda. *Gambling: Who Wins? Who Loses?* Amherst, N.Y.: Prometheus Books, 2003.

Overview of main trends in gambling and legal, economic, political, social and ethical issues.

Young, Kimberly S., and Cristiano Nabuco de Abreu. *Internet Addiction: A Handbook and Guide to Evaluation and Treatment.* Hoboken, N.J.: John Wiley & Sons, 2010.

Provides a framework to understand Internet addiction.

DOCUMENTARIES AND DVDS

Addiction Advocacy. National Council on Alcoholism and Drug Dependence, 2006.

Discusses concept of addiction and how it affects one's personal life.

Cyberwar. Frontline, 2003.

Discusses cyberthreats and Internet society.

Digital Nation: Life on the Frontier. PBS, 2010.

Compelling stories about Internet addiction.

Media Addiction. Reel Grrls Television, 2009

Youth-produced film exploring how people are attached to media.

WEB SITES

Academy of Interactive Arts and Sciences
http://www.interactive.org

Professional membership organization that serves the entertainment software community.

American Gaming Association
http://www.americangaming.org

Teaches community members about casino entertainment through education and advocacy.

American Mental Health Counselors Association
http://www.amhca.org

Provides mental health support and counseling information.

Center for Democracy and Technology
http://www.cdt.org

Working to keep the Internet open, innovative, and free.

Center for Disease Control and Prevention
http://www.cdc.gov

Provides mental health and medical support information.

The Center for Internet Addiction
http://www.netaddiction.com

Resources for those addicted to the Net.

The Center for Information Security Awareness
http://www.cfisa.org

Works to increase security awareness among various community members.

The Children's Internet Protection Act (CIPA)

http://www.fcc.gov/guides/childrens-internet-protection-act

Federal law that addresses offensive content viewable on school and library computers.

Cyberbully 411

http://www.cyberbully411.org

Educational materials for youth on cyberbullying.

Cyberbullying Research Center

http://www.cyberbullying.us/resources.php

Identifies the causes and consequences of online victimization.

The Cyber Safety and Ethics Initiative

http://www.rrcsei.org/

Ensures cybersafety among parents, educators and youth.

Department of Motor Vehicles

http://www.dmv.com

Easy-to-understand articles about laws pertaining to IT devices and driving.

Digital Games Research Association (DiGRA)

http://www.digra.org

Worldwide organization that focus on digital games.

Electronic Privacy Information Center

http://epic.org

Keeps community members informed about privacy and civil liberties issues.

Entertainment Software Rating Board (ESRB)

http://www.esrb.org

Nonprofit organization that rates all sorts of games.

The Family Online Safety Institute
http://www.fosi.org
Promotes best practices in the area of online safety with respect to free expression.

Federal Bureau of Investigation Kids Page
http://www.fbi.gov/fungames/kids/kids
Covers investigation, safety, and other kids' topics.

Federal Communications Commision (FCC)
http://www.fcc.gov
Regulates interstate and international communications.

Harvard Medical School: Division on Addictions
http://www.divisiononaddictions.org
Research in the area of online addictions, gambling, and gaming.

Identity Theft Resource Center (ITRC)
http://www.idtheftcenter.org
National organization for identity theft.

Interactive Gaming Council (IGC)
http://www.igcouncil.org
Provides a forum to advocate for the interactive gaming industry.

The International Game Developers Association
http://www.igda.org
Organization that advocates issues pertaining to digital game creation.

The Internet Keep Safe Coalition
http://ikeepsafe.org
Collaboration of professionals to disseminate safety resources to families worldwide.

i-SAFE Inc.

http://www.isafe.org

Nonprofit dedicated to protecting online activity experienced by youth.

The National Center for Missing and Exploited Children

http://www.missingkids.com

Provides information and resources on issues regarding missing and exploited children.

The National Center for Victims of Crime

http://www.ncvc.org

Assists victims with support after being victimized.

The National Council on Problem Gambling

http://www.ncpgambling.org

Offers referral resources including self-help guides and local and state information.

National Crime Prevention Council

http://www.ncpc.org

Provides resources for cyberbullying and Internet safety.

National Cyber Security Alliance

http://www.staysafeonline.org

Supports digital citizens that utilize the Internet.

NetSmartz Workshop

http://www.netsmartz.org

Educates families and professionals about Internet concerns.

OnGuardOnline

http://onguardonline.gov

Provides tips to help prevent computer crimes.

The Pew Research Center's Internet and American Life Project
http://www.pewinternet.org
Provides information on online safety and education.

Stop Bullying
http://www.stopbullying.gov
Disseminates information from government agencies about bullying to increase awareness, prevention, and intervention.

United States Computer Emergency Readiness Team (US-CERT)
http://www.us-cert.gov
Interacts with government entities, industry, and the community to defend against cyberattacks.

Working to Halt Abuse Online (WHO@)
http://www.haltabuse.org
Resources for victims of online abuse.

Wired Safety
http://wiredsafety.org
Educational resources for online safety

INDEX

Pages numbers in *italics* indicate photos or illustrations.

A

accidents, while texting 28–30
action-adventure games 54–55
addiction. *See also* Internet addiction
   biology in 32–33
   causes of 31–36
   chemistry in 22, 32–33
   coexisting 22–23
   definition of 11, 21, 25
   direct harms of 100, 102–106, 116
   disease model of 32–33
   economic harms of 27–30
   emotional causes of 35
   environment in 35–36
   indirect harms of 100, 102–106, 116
   nature of 16–17
   psychology in 35
   recovering from 68
   social harms of 27–30
   syndrome model of 21–22, *23*, 33, 36
   tertiary harms of 100, 109–110, 116
adults
   gaming by 56–57, *57*
   Internet use by 38, 42
   social computing by 42
advertising
   sexual content in 95
   in Web 3.0 48
alcohol, sales to minors 91–92
Alexander, Ben *123*
American Civil Liberties Union 96
American Medical Association 127
American Psychological Association (APA) 24
attitudes, in addiction 30–31

B

Barbie Fashion Show 55
behaviors
   environment in 35–36

in Internet addiction 30–31
biochemistry, in addiction 22, 67
biology, in addiction 33
BlackBerries, as "crackberries" 16
Black Friday 90–91
Block, Jerald 24–25
brain activity, in online gaming 34
bullying 111–112, 113–114

C

camps, abuse at 124–125
Caplan, Scott 66
casinos, online 74, 105–106
casual games 55
Caught in the Net (Young) 118–119
cell phones
   banned while driving 88–89, *89*
   computing on 84–85
   daily reliance on 14
   excessive use of 84–89
   popularity of 84, 86–87
Center for Internet Addiction Recovery 64
chat, online, sex-related 47
chemical addiction 21, 25–26, 32–33
Child Online Protection Act 96
Children's Internet Protection Act 96
cigarettes, addiction to 32–33
classmates, negative effects on 108
cognitive behavioral therapy 121
Communications Decency Act 96
compulsive shopping. *See* shopping, online, compulsive
consequences 12–14, 100–106
   direct harms 100, 102–106, 116
   indirect harms 100, 106–109, 116
   tertiary harms 100, 109–110, 116
copyright, pirating and 53
coworkers, negative effects on 108–109
"crackberries" 16
criminals, technology used by 8–9
Ctrl+Alt+Del (web comic) 66
culture
   definition of 38–39
   gambling in 70, *71*

154

ABOUT THE AUTHORS

DR. SAMUEL C. MCQUADE, III currently serves as the professional studies graduate program coordinator in the Center for Multidisciplinary Studies at the Rochester Institute of Technology. He holds a doctoral degree in public policy from George Mason University, and a master's degree in public administration from the University of Washington. He teaches and conducts research at RIT in areas inclusive of computer crime, enterprise security and career options in high-tech societies.

In January 2008, he concluded a massive cybercrime victimization and offending survey of over 40,000 K–12th grade students along with hundreds of parents and teachers. Results revealed new understanding of ways in which youth behave and interact online frequently by abusing computerized systems and devices.

Dr. McQuade has presented his research findings from this and other studies, along with implications for Internet safety, information security and cyberethics, at major events hosted by: the American Society of Criminology, the British Society of Criminology, the U.S. Department of Homeland Security, the National Intelligence Council, the National Governors Association, the Berkman Center for Internet and Society at Harvard Law School, the Family Online Safety Institute, the Division on Addictions of Harvard Medical School, and the National Association of State Chief Information Officers. His other books include *Understanding and Managing Cybercrime* (Pearson, 2006), *The Encyclopedia of Cybercrime* (Greenwood, 2009) *Cyber Bullying: Protecting Kids and Adults from Online Bullies* (Greenwood, 2009),

SARAH E. GENTRY, M.S., is currently a graduate student in the professional studies master's of science degree program at the Rochester Institute of Technology with course concentrations in security technology management and business. Sarah serves as a graduate research assistant for the RIT-led Cyber Safety and Ethics Initiative. She has worked as a system administrator for both the RIT residential computing lab and the Society for the Protection and Care of Children in Rochester, N.Y. Sarah holds a bachelor's of applied arts and science degree in multidisciplinary studies and is currently coauthoring three separate children's educational books pertaining to using the Internet and information technologies safely and responsibly.

DR. JAMES P. COLT, ED.D., is the coordinator of school safety and security for the Monroe 1 BOCES (Board of Cooperative Educational Services). He is a former police officer employed by the State University of New York, and also served as a criminal justice instructor and school community safety specialist at Monroe 1 BOCES. He also is a certified public school teacher and school administrator in New York State. He earned a master's degree in criminal justice from Buffalo State College, and also holds a master's degree in educational administration from St. John Fisher College. He also earned his doctorate from St. John Fisher College, with a research focus on cyberbullying and cyberoffending. He also serves on the executive committee of the Cyber Safety and Ethics Initiative in western New York. He is a frequent presenter at conferences and workshops on topics related to cybersafety, bullying, violence prevention and crisis intervention, and emergency preparedness.

MARCUS K. ROGERS, PH.D., is the director of the Cyber Forensics Program in the department of computer and information technology at Purdue University, a former police officer, and the editor in chief of the *Journal of Digital Forensic Practice.* He has written, edited, and reviewed numerous articles and books on cybercrime. He is a professor, university faculty scholar, and research faculty member at the Center for Education and Research in Information Assurance and Security. He also is the international chair of the Law, Compliance and Investigation Domain of the Common Body of Knowledge (CBK) committee, chair of the Ethics Committee for the Digital and Multimedia Sciences section of the American Academy of Forensic Sciences, and chair of the Certification and Test Committee–Digital Forensics Certification Board. As a police officer he worked in the area of fraud and computer crime investigations. Dr. Rogers sits on the editorial board for several professional journals. He is also a member of various national and international committees focusing on digital forensic science and digital evidence. Dr. Rogers is the author of books, book chapters, and journal publications in the field of digital forensics and applied psychological analysis. His research interests include applied cyberforensics, psychological digital crime scene analysis, cybercrime scene analysis, and cyber-terrorism. He is a frequent speaker at international and national information assurance and security conferences, and guest lectures throughout the world.